THE DRAVIDIAN ELEMENT IN INDIAN CULTURE

THE DRAVIDIAN ELEMENT IN INDIAN CULTURE

GILBERT SLATER

GYAN

Published by

GYAN

Gyan Publishing House
5, Ansari Road
Daryaganj, New Delhi-110002
Phone: 011-47034999, 9811692060
E-mail: books@gyanbooks.com

Distribution Network
gyanbooks.com
India, USA, Canada, UK, Australia

ISBN: 978-93-7097-210-0 (PB)

First Published, 1924

2nd Impression 2025

Printed at: Gyan Press, Delhi.

THE DRAVIDIAN ELEMENT IN INDIAN CULTURE
Author: GILBERT SLATER

THE DRAVIDIAN ELEMENT IN INDIAN CULTURE

THE DRAVIDIAN ELEMENT IN INDIAN CULTURE

By GILBERT SLATER, M.A., D.Sc.

LATE PROFESSOR OF INDIAN ECONOMICS IN THE UNIVERSITY OF MADRAS

1924

PREFACE

In the summer of 1915, having been notified that the Syndicate of the University of Madras had recommended my appointment to the Chair of Indian Economics, I began the study of Tamil. This gave me the first suggestion of doubt with regard to the soundness of the theory, prevalent both in Europe and in India, of the Aryan origin of Indian culture. Those doubts were strengthened on my arrival in Madras by discussion with Mr H. V. Lanchester, who was then advising the Government of Madras in the subject of Town Planning, who, besides giving me much other interesting information, showed me a striking series of photographs of Sivaganga. During my residence in South India, which lasted till the spring of 1922, the question of the origin of Dravidian civilisation and of the extent of the Dravidian contribution to the totality of Indian culture was continually in my mind, and I seized many opportunities of discussing aspects of the question with anyone I met who was also interested in it. By degrees the opinions which are set out in the following pages formed themselves. It was not, however, till after my return to England in 1922 that I became acquainted with the work of Elliot Smith, Perry, and others of the diffusionist school of anthropology and archæology, most of which was only published after I had gone to India, where knowledge of new books outside my special subject did not often reach me.

The first unfinished draft of this book was written in India in 1920. For the stimulus to take up the task of completing it I am indebted in the first instance to Dr E. E. Power, and later to Prof. Fleure. I am further indebted to Prof. Fleure, and also to Prof. G. Elliot Smith, for very kindly reading the typescript and proofs and for making valuable suggestions, of which some only are specifically acknowledged in the text.

There is one small detail in the valuable note to Chapter I, so kindly supplied by Prof. Fleure, with which I am not in entire agreement. He regards the land routes connecting India with Mesopotamia as probably more important in the conveyance of culture elements than the sea route. I am inclined to think the sea route as, on the whole, probably the more important, partly on *a priori* grounds, partly on account of that very significant fact "Eridu sank into insignificance with the retreat of the shore line." This suggests, though it of course does not prove, that the maritime trade of Babylonia in the third millennium B.C. was of great importance, much greater than any possible caravan trade. After passing through the Persian Gulf the maritime trade route must have divided, westwards along the coast of Arabia, southwards and eastwards along the coast of India, and the two branches may well have been of approximately equal importance.

I also am inclined to follow Elliot Smith in assigning more importance to maritime contact between Egypt and India than Prof. Fleure would apparently be disposed to endorse; and I fancy I differ slightly from both in estimating somewhat more highly the importance of the possible backward conveyance of culture elements from India westwards, and the independent achievements of pre-Aryan India, and of post-Aryan Dravidian India.

GILBERT SLATER

CONTENTS

LIST OF ILLUSTRATIONS

THE DRAVIDIAN ELEMENT IN INDIAN CULTURE

CHAPTER I

THE DRAVIDIANS

THE word "Dravidian" indicates a linguistic rather than a racial section of the people of India. The Sanscrit word "Dravida" means "southern,"[1] and the Dravidian languages are, broadly, the languages of Southern India. The 1911 census recognises fifteen of them spoken by over sixty-two million people. Tamil is the most cultured, and also the purest, and is spoken by over eighteen million people in India, as well as by many in Ceylon, and by Tamilian emigrants in Assam,

[1] According to some philologists. Some maintain that it is derived from "Tamir" (Tamil), and others have followed Dr Caldwell's theory that "Tamir" is derived from "Dravida."

Burma, Malaysia, etc. It is the language of the Carnatic from Madras to Cape Comorin. Andhra, or Telugu, spoken by some twenty-four million people, is the language of the Carnatic and Northern Circars from Madras to Ganjam; Canarese (ten and a half millions) has a great range on the Deccan and is the official language of the state of Mysore; Malayalam is the language of Travancore, Cochin, and Malabar, and is spoken by some seven millions. These are the four chief Dravidian languages. Each of the three last has borrowed words to a much larger extent than Tamil from Sanscritic languages. The remaining eleven Dravidian languages have no literary importance.

To the general rule that Dravidian languages belong to the south of India there is one remarkable exception. Brahui is isolated and far separated from its kin, having its locale in Baluchistan. The tribes that speak Brahui resemble to a considerable extent the people of South India in physical characteristics and temperament, and show a marked contrast to their neighbours, so that it is clear that in their case affinity of language is the result of affinity of race. This is a fact of considerable significance in reference to the question of Dravidian origins. But in India proper it is impossible to find any definite ethnological boundary between the Dravidians of the south and other Indian people. Apart from jungle tribes there is a gradual transition of average type from the extreme south-east to the extreme north-west. Apart from certain fishing castes and certain primitive hill and jungle tribes, which latter are hypothetically classed by some as proto-Dravidians, and by others, perhaps more accurately, as pre-Dravidians, and who appear to have acquired Dravidian languages by contact with Dravidian neighbours, the various folk who speak Dravidian languages show close racial affinity among themselves. This justifies us in using what would otherwise be the question begging term " the Dravidian Race," which we may define as including nearly all the people who now speak Dravidian languages, and vast numbers of other Indians who now speak Sanscritic languages imposed upon them by conquering tribes. For the fact that Sanscritic languages have pushed the Dravidian languages, with the exception of Brahui, into the extreme south of India is no reason for supposing that the "Aryan" conquerors who spoke Sanscrit exterminated or expelled the Dravidians in or from the rest of India, any more than the fact that French is a romance language is evidence to show that Cæsar's legions exterminated the Celtic-speaking inhabitants of Gaul. In the struggle for existence between two languages which must ensue in such circumstances the issue is determined, partly by circumstances, and partly by the characteristics of the languages. In Gaul, Latin was under a disadvantage through being the language of a small minority; but it survived by virtue, on the one hand, of being the language of the conquerors, and, on the other, by being easier to learn than any Gaelic or Brythonic language.

The struggle for existence between Sanscritic and Dravidian tongues over a great part of India must have been a close parallel. All the Dravidian languages are extremely difficult. How much more difficult they are than Sanscritic languages may be estimated from the fact that where they are the vernaculars the language of communication between European employers and Indian servants is almost invariably English, whereas in the rest of India it is Hindustani. In Madras, when the Buckingham and Carnatic cotton mills were established under European management, it was soon decided to set up schools to teach half-timers and children of operatives English, as the only effective alternative to dependence on native interpreters. It is clear, therefore, that whenever and wherever any small body of Aryan invaders established themselves as a ruling caste in a district populated by Dravidians, while they became merged in the native population, their Sanscritic language would become the language of the district. The supersession of Dravidian languages by Sanscritic is still proceeding wherever the two come into contact. The facts with regard to the distribution of languages therefore are quite in harmony with the conclusions indicated by the ethnological evidence, that the Dravidian element preponderates over all other elements in the racial make-up of the people of India. It is also to be noted that the phonetic system of Sanscrit itself is intermediate between that of Tamil and other Dravidian languages on one hand, and that of other Indo-Germanic languages on the other. This indicates that even when the Rig-Veda took the form in which it has come down to us a considerable part of the Sanscrit-speaking population was of Dravidian race.

Who, then, are the Dravidians? What racial affinities have they with populations outside India? How did they come?

After much controversy it is now, I believe, generally agreed that the main racial element in the Dravidian population is a branch of the Mediterranean race, if that term be understood in its most extended sense, or at least a closely allied race. My own somewhat crude and amateurish observation is that the resemblances in shape of skull, colour and texture of hair, colour of eyes, in features and build, are striking. The most obvious and well-marked difference is in colour of skin, which in the Dravidians is, on the average, much darker, ranging from a fairness equal to that of the average Italian or Spanish complexion nearly to a negro black. There is also a wider range in texture of hair, high degrees of fuzziness and of smoothness being approached; and a rather larger proportion of faces with thick lips and broad noses than among typical Mediterranean folk. All these deviations from the Mediterranean type seemed to me to be easily explained on the hypothesis that after the Dravidians entered India some inter-breeding took place between them and the dark and thick-lipped primitive "pre-Dravidian" races still surviving in the jungles.[1] In this way the Dravidians may be presumed to have acquired a characteristic of great survival value for life in the tropics in variability of skin colouration; while losing something in average beauty of feature, particularly among the Tamils. There is an unkind proverb current among the Anglo-Indians (old sense) of Madras, that "God made the Tamil woman in answer to the prayer 'Lead us not into temptation.'" It is an exaggeration of the fact that the Tamils, the most southerly of the Dravidians, are on the average somewhat less pleasing in feature, as well as somewhat darker in complexion, than the Telugus, Canarese, and Malayalis. The further south we go the larger the proportion of pre-Dravidian blood among the agricultural population, and those castes to which the official designation of "Adi Dravidas" has been

[1] See note at end of chapter.

assigned are probably predominantly pre-Dravidian.

The working of the forces of selection on Dravidian colouration diverges in two directions. Among the mass of the people who must needs labour in the sun, and for whom the most comfortable costume for men is a small loincloth and a turban, sufficient protective pigment in the skin is most helpful, and hence natural selection tends to approximate the colouration to that of the negro. But on the other hand, among all Dravidians, as among other Indians, fair complexions are much admired. On the stage the boys or young men who impersonate the heroines take great pains to whiten their faces, and achieve an effect that is painful to European eyes. The fairer a girl the more eligible she is in marriage; matrimonial advertisements, whether inserted by would-be bridegrooms or by fathers of marriageable girls, invariably bear witness to this fact, and in respectable circles the fairer the daughter the smaller the "bridegroom price" her father has to pay to his prospective son-in-law to secure the marriage. There is therefore a tendency towards fairness among the privileged classes. These divergent forces are no doubt largely, though probably not wholly, accountable for the fact that the very name for caste in Sanscrit primarily means colour, and that the social grading of the different castes agrees very closely with their grading in inverse order of average darkness of colour.

Assuming, then, that the Dravidians are one section of the great Mediterranean race, modified by the intermixture of alien blood here suggested, we must conclude that they migrated into India at some far distant date from their original home.[1] The logical alternative, that the Mediterranean race itself originated in India, is distinctly improbable, though it has been alleged by some Tamil writers that Tamil traditions indicate that the original Dra-

[1] The "Mediterranean race" probably came from East Africa, whence possibly some of them wandered via Arabia and South Persia to India.—G. ELLIOT SMITH.

vidian home was in land that once made a bridge connecting Southern India with Africa, at a time when the present Indo-Gangetic plain was sea. The extreme antiquity of the Mediterranean race in Egypt, and the fact that it is to all appearances in much closer harmony with its environment in the Mediterranean basin than the Dravidians are in South India, seem to be conclusive. It has been a cause of frequent surprise to me to find how kindly students from Madras take to the English climate, and how little they differed from me in toleration of the midday heat of their own city.

By what route, then, did they come? Prof. Grafton Elliot Smith, in "Migrations of Early Culture" (p. 80), says, "The bringers of the new culture" (*i.e.* seafarers from the west, who, as he believes, from the third millennium and especially in the period about 800 B.C. carried the "heliolithic" culture, mainly evolved in Egypt, but with elements gathered elsewhere, far and wide along the coasts of the Old World and the New) "mingled their blood with the aboriginal pre-Dravidian population, and the result was the Dravidians."[1] But the western sailors, pearl and shell fishers, and metallurgists, could have spared very few men and far fewer, if any, women for settlement in any particular portion of the enormous length of seacoast which, according to the Professor himself, they visited and on which they left a deep cultural impress. The hypothesis, therefore, assuming a relatively late date, does not allow sufficient time for the growth of a great Dravidian population, of mixed western and aboriginal descent, but approximating in physical and mental characteristics much more closely to its immigrant than to its aboriginal ancestors, before the Aryan invasions, even if we assign to the latter the latest possible date. The Dravidians must have come to India long before 800, or 900, or even 1000 B.C.

[1] This is a very loose statement. The admixture of people of "Mediterranean" race with Pre-Dravidian occurred many centuries before the coming of the Stone Culture.—G. E. S.

Mr W. J. Perry ("The Children of the Sun," p. 560) gives evidence for thinking that carriers of Egyptian culture frequented Indian shores from the time of the Sixth Dynasty (*cir.* 2600 B.C.) onwards. Elliot Smith in "Ancient Mariners" (1917) also adopted this earlier date. In this form it becomes more probable, but I can only accept it with a further modification.[1] If it is rejected, land routes through Afghanistan and Baluchistan have to be considered. With regard to these the present location of the Brahuis[2] along the eastern boundary of the latter country is perhaps a sufficient reason for ruling out the Afghan route ending in the Khyber Pass. This leaves two possible routes, one following the route suggested for a railway to link

[1] See page 158.

[2] The hypothesis has been suggested that the Brahuis migrated into Baluchistan from the South, see, for example, Dr Konow's article, "Dravidian," in *Ency. Brit.*, 11th Edition. No possible explanation for such a movement from the fertile south country, while it still had room to spare, into a very distant and inhospitable mountain region has ever been put forward. Discussion seems unnecessary.

Mesopotamia with India, crossing Baluchistan from the Persian Gulf in a north-easterly direction to Quetta, and then turning southwards through the Bolan Pass; the other following the seacoast to the mouth of the River Indus. The Brahui country lies between these two routes, but more closely adjacent to the latter, and this on the whole appears to me the more probable. We know enough of the progress of desiccation of all the land between Mesopotamia and India during historic times to have some confidence in inferring that there was sufficient water, vegetation, and game, to draw hunting and fishing tribes, as I conceive the Dravidians to have been when on this march, continually forwards. This would make the coming of the Dravidians analogous to the first movements of the Phœnicians, who, according to their own traditions, starting from the Persian Gulf, spread along the shores of Arabia to the Red Sea before establishing themselves on the Palestinian coast. Arabia perhaps even then offered little temptation to leave the shore and settle inland ; but from the west coast of India the river Indus, the later caravan and present railway routes from the Gulf of Cambay to the Upper Ganges, and the Palghat Gap were geographical invitations to migrate to the most fertile plains.

With regard to the date of this migration, if, as will be contended below, Dravidian culture was evolved *in India*, and mainly under the stimulus of the Indian environment, though not without the operation of important external influences, then we have to note :—

(1) That a journey from some part of the Mediterranean basin through Baluchistan into India almost necessarily implies a journey through Mesopotamia ; and

(2) that under the supposed conditions this journey must have *preceded* the dawn of Sumerian civilisation.

If the Dravidians, after passing through Babylonia, brought no knowledge of agriculture with them into India, they must have passed through Babylonia before agriculture was practised there; if on the other hand they did bring that knowledge with them, the reverse must be the case.

In the necessary lack of any definite knowledge on the subject, we are tempted to speculate on the causes of this and similar migrations among people in the hunting stage. Though migration is relatively easy for them, even in their case it is unlikely that it would take place without some impelling reason. Leaving aside the question of climatic changes, the suggestion may be deemed worth consideration that such a motive might arise through the acquisition of improved apparatus for hunting. Suppose, for example, the invention of the bow and arrow is achieved (as presumably it must have been) at some particular spot in a vast district wherein hitherto no better tool was known for killing animals than the spear and throwing-stick. The first temporary effect would be that ampler supplies of meat would be obtained from the same hunting grounds, and this would lead to an excess of births over deaths. But later on the increased efficiency in the methods of killing game would lead to a diminution in the numbers available to be killed, and the users of the new apparatus would be obliged to push out in any possible direction to find fresh hunting grounds. Since what will kill a deer will kill a man, neighbouring tribes who had failed to adopt the new weapon would be unable to stop the movement; and those that did adopt it would be impelled to join in the migration. As a general principle of the causes underlying migrations of hunting tribes this hypothesis seems to harmonise with the great mass of information which has been so industriously put together with regard to movements of races and cultures in Europe in the pre-agricultural period. Cultural movements have taken place sometimes independently of, and sometimes associated with, racial migrations; and when these have taken place in association the new immigrants have brought with them something new and serviceable in the hunt, as, for example, the people of Mediterranean race and Azilian culture spreading northwards and bringing the use of the bow and arrow; and the people of the Maglemosian culture working westwards and bringing the hunting dog.

It seems more probable than not that some such advance in the means and methods of hunting was the cause of the Dravidian immigration into India.

Some dim and uncertain light upon the sort of mentality that characterised those ancient Dravidian hunters is supplied by the existing languages. The Tamil language, being the purest, is the one we turn to; but as it is known to us it is the product of a very long period of a somewhat elaborate civilisation. Nevertheless the mentality which produced that civilisation, and perfected the language, must have been inherited by the cultured Dravidians from their hunting ancestors, if only possessed by the latter in an undeveloped state.

The Tamil language is extraordinary in its subtlety and sense of logic. It is termed agglutinative, but it may equally well be described as at the initial inflexional stage. There are personal terminations to verbs, but these are easily recognisable modifications of the personal pronouns: *e.g.* he, she, and it are respectively ăvăn, ăvăl, and ădu; the terminations of a verb in any tense in the third person singular are ān, āl, and ădu. Nouns and pronouns have case terminations, which again in many cases are recognisable as separate words. Broadly it may be said that all nouns are declined identically, and all case terminations are the same in the singular and plural, the plural having the additional plural suffix. The subtlety of the Dravidian mind is illustrated by the manner in which a negative form of the verb is obtained. To make a present tense the appropriate present suffix must be added to the verbal root; similarly for past and future; if then to the verbal root the personal pronoun is added without any connecting time suffix, the action denoted by the verb is neither present, past, or future, *i.e.* it is denied. E.g. *cey* is *do*; *cey-girr-ēn* (present), I do; *cey-d-ēn*, I did; *cey-v-ēn*, I shall do; but *ceyy-ēn* (an extra y for euphony) is I do not, I did not, I shall not do. This, while both ingenious and logical, does not exhaust all the grades of negative meaning which may be required; accordingly Tamil, by the help of the word *illai* (not), has in addition a negative like ours, in which the person and tense are defined; another negative in which the tense is defined but not the person; and a perfectly general negative in which neither tense nor person is defined.

Similarly with regard to interrogative sentences. There is an enclitic *-ā*, equal to the Latin *-ne*, which may be attached to any word in a sentence; and another enclitic -ō, which, like the Latin *num*, asks a question incredulously, but which also can be attached to any word. If the sense of the Latin *nonne* is required, the word *illai* can be introduced, but the enclitic

-*ā* or -*ō* is not attached to *illai*, but to the word which expresses the precise point of the question. The system of interrogatives, in a word, is as perfect as could be formed by the human mind.

Another feature of the language is its extraordinary richness in honorifics, and in the use of the honorific plural in the third person as well as the second. This feature in particular we may attribute to the social organisation of later times, with its despotic monarchs, ceremonial courts, and priestly caste. Tamil versification is based on quantity, like Greek and Latin; it also employs rime, but at the beginnings, not the endings of verses; and alliteration, but within the verse, and not as a link between verses. Tamil music is based upon quarter-tones, *i.e.* there are twenty-eight divisions of the octave instead of seven.

Indian culture, with its special characteristic of systematic and subtle philosophical thought, must have come from people capable of originating and developing it.

That capacity would naturally be exhibited also in the evolution of language, and the purest Dravidian language does exhibit it in the highest degree—in a higher degree than any other Indian language.

NOTE BY PROF. FLEURE

THE RACIAL AFFINITIES OF SOUTH INDIA AND EARLY CULTURAL CONTACTS

THE heads of the people of South India vary considerably, but towards the end of the peninsula are often very long and narrow and rather high. Save in a few localities heads are generally long in Dravidian India. Analogous types, with fairer skins as a rule, occur here and there in South-west Asia, and there can be no doubt about the structural analogies with Semitic types in Arabia, apart from colour and nasal features, and Hamitic types in North Africa as well as the average Mediterranean types around the western basin of the Great Sea.

In all the groups one finds individuals who by their extremely long narrow high heads, their short broad noses and prominent mouths (often with thick lips) advertise their descent from such ancient types as are preserved for our inspection from the lower layer of the Grimaldi cave and from Combe Capelle in France. It is widely held that the modern racial stocks between the Iberian Peninsula and the Deccan are largely the result of evolution from ancient types nearly resembling those just mentioned, and that, under diversity of environmental influences, the course of evolution has been to some extent divergent. In South-west Asia, with the periods of cold, a large nose, capable of warming the air on its way down to the lungs, has come into existence, and with it a general emphasis of the profile. In North Africa and in the Deccan the tropical sun has apparently been a factor of high development of pigment and of a certain looseness of skin pores, carrying with it a frequent tendency to fuzziness of the hair. But in Africa the full negro has completed his evolution in the broad region to the south of the Hamitic belt, while the Deccan narrows to nothing on its south side. The milder, cooler conditions of the Mediterranean and a good deal of contact with the peoples of Northern and North-western Europe has led to a lesser development of pigmentation and probably to a greater regularity of facial features.

During palæolithic times in Europe it seems probable that for long spells the Sahara, Arabia, Persia, and Turkestan were far more hospitable to man than they have since become, following the northward spread of climatic belts as the European ice sheets of the Ice Age diminished. Long-headed man, with some pigment, and most often a high as well as a very long head, and a short broad nose, may be supposed to have lived all over a zone stretching from the Iberian Peninsula through North Africa and South-west Asia to the Deccan at least.

With the change of climate just mentioned came not only a serious, if incomplete, separation of western Mediterranean, Sudanese (Hamitic), Semitic (the wetter lands round the fringe of Arabia), Iranian, and Indian provinces, but also a pressure of men into such relatively attractive areas as those just given.

In the case of each area we thus find remnants of ancient types along with types which trend towards what anthropologists call for convenience Mediterranean, Hamitic, Semitic, Iranian, and Dravidian groups. Each group shows evolution towards characteristics adapted to the circumstances of its region. There is thus in each case a considerable variation, as well as a considerable evidence of a common foundation for all these groups, and for others which need not concern us here.

It will also be obvious that the Mediterranean group, for example, shows links with African groups, and might almost be said to grade from the Hamitic, the two having suffered evolution from not very dissimilar beginnings. In the same way Semitic, Iranian, and Dravidian, or Southern Indian, show gradations from one to another, and as South India is in large measure the terminus of the movement, on the one hand gradations within it are strongly marked, and on the other hand links with regions further west are fairly obvious.

In Europe, from the dawn of the Neolithic period, we get evidence of many inventions tending towards the enrichment of life. The domestication of plants and animals suggests the better development of a home and of soft food for babies, and this is followed in its turn by the development of pottery, of wedge-shaped stone axes for tree cutting, of the wheel, and so of much of the technical equipment of civilisation, coupled with an improvement in weapons. These improvements in varying degrees were carried by the peoples pressing out of the regions which became arid. That the coastal belt of Baluchistan may have been a zone of movement at that time is rendered likely by the persistence of the Brahui behind it.

When one considers the subsequent enormous development of culture in the lower Euphrates and Tigris regions it becomes permissible to suggest that from time immemorial Mesopotamian influences have probably had their effect upon Dravidian civilisation evolving in India.

Until recently it was the general view that prior to about 800 B.C. communication by sea was very limited. The discoveries in connection with Minoan culture showing links of Crete with pre-dynastic Egypt and the Sumer of the third millennium B.C., as well as the more intensive study of west European archæology, have shown that maritime communications were developed far earlier than had been supposed, and were fairly considerable even during the third millennium B.C.

Sumerian legends locate Paradise, where the gods first blessed mankind with the manners of civilised life, in Dilmun, on the shore of the Persian Gulf. In the Island Bushire M. Pezard found traces of neolithic culture and thin monochrome pottery decorated in geometrical style, characteristic of the earliest cultures at Susa, Musyan, Ur, and Eridu. It was the date-palm that made possible the rapid rise of the Sumerian people once they reached this region from the upper Tigris. Dilmun is mentioned in their records as a land of the date. The origins of the painted pottery in Elam and Sumer date back beyond 4000 B.C., and Susa developed greatly about that date, while information from tablets occurs for dates from 3200 B.C. onwards. Sargon (*cir.* 2800 B.C.) seems to have had relations with Cyprus.[1] Eridu and Lagash in early times were practically sea-board cities, but Eridu sank into insignificance after the age of Hammurabi (*cir.* 2100 B.C.) with the retreat of the shore line. These facts suggest the possibility of ancient culture connections between Mesopotamia and India, though there is as yet little direct dateable evidence.

A feature of Indian archæology to which special attention has been drawn by Grafton Elliot Smith (" Migrations of Early Culture ") and W. J. Perry (" Children of the Sun ") is the occurrence of megaliths on the Deccan said to be related to metallic deposits.[2] This group of megaliths seems to be related on the one hand to analogous remains towards the Pacific, and on the other to monuments south of the Caspian, in Georgia towards the Euxine, in the Crimea, and in Thrace. Perry thinks this maritime intercourse affected India about the middle of the third millennium, but the distribution of the megaliths suggests that land routes have also to be considered, and the evidence of the Brahui supports the idea of land routes

[1] See "Cambridge Ancient History," Vol. I., ch. x. (1923).

[2] Note also the occurrence of dolmens and kist-væns near Trichur in Cochin, indicating the use of the route of the Palghat Gap.—G. S.

as well as sea ones. We thus have the suggestion of rather highly developed culture from the already old-established Mesopotamian civilisations probably affecting Dravidian India about 2500 B.C., if not still earlier. The broad-headed fishing castes of the south-west and south-east coasts of India, pointed out by Hornell,[1] is a point to be borne in mind for future investigation in connection with the occurrence of broad-headed men along so many coastal stretches in West and South-west Europe connected with early maritime trade.

Summing up, therefore, we may picture survivors of early man in India influenced from the dawn of Neolithic time by immigrations of long heads, akin to those termed Mediterranean, Hamitic, and Semitic, pressed out of the lands of increasing aridity; and that these immigrations may well have brought to India many improvements, lifting men above the merely hunting stage, and even giving the beginnings of agriculture. The growth of long-distance communications, which was such a general feature of the life of the third millennium B.C., can scarcely fail to have left its mark upon India, the three routes with the west to be considered being—(1) the sea route from Mesopotamia following the coast of the Persian Gulf and the Arabian Sea; (2) the land routes from Mesopotamia to India, and (3) the sea route from the Egyptian ports on the Red Sea and the Land of Punt following the southern coast of Arabia as described in the "Periplus of the Erythræan Sea." It seems justifiable to use the hypothesis that the

[1] At British Association, Liverpool, 1923.

PLATE I. CROMLECH, CHINGLEPUT

culture elements which thus reached India, probably not less than a thousand years before the coming of the Aryans, interwove themselves with the earlier achievements of the higher races among the populations already settled in India, and that the Dravidian culture is the result.

H. J. F.

[Prof. Fleure adds:—"These notes were originally supplied to the author for his consideration. The materials on which they are based may be traced through reference to Giuffrida Ruggeri, 'Outlines of a Systematic Anthropology of Asia' (Calcutta, 1921), to the 'Cambridge Ancient History' (Vol. I., 1923), and to H. J. Fleure's papers in the *Journal of the Royal Anthropological Institute* (1916, 1918, 1921), and in 'Man.'"]

CHAPTER II

THE ARYANS

THE great obstacle to a right appreciation of the Dravidian influence in the evolution of Indian culture is the wide currency and established position of what may be called "the Aryan myth." Indians cling to the theory that they are "Aryans," and that their religion and culture are "Aryan." The word "Aryan" is legitimate enough, provided the definite meaning is attached to it, as a name for the invaders from the north-west who introduced the Sanscrit language into India. It is illegitimate if used to imply the theory popularised by Max Müller, that an ancient "Aryan" race of men, superior to other races, spread from the original "Aryan home" somewhere in Europe or Asia, over India, Persia, and Europe, displacing the previous occupants, all regarded as inferior mentally, physically, and culturally, and bequeathing to their descendants the various languages of the Indo-Germanic family. All attempts to harmonise that theory with the facts have broken down hopelessly, and Max Müller himself was brought to admit that language is no test of race. Nevertheless it lingers on even in Europe. H. G. Wells, in his "History of Mankind," talks of "Nordic Aryans," though it is perfectly obvious that, whatever the racial affinities of the Aryans might have been, they could not have been characterised by the blue eyes and blond complexions which mark the Nordic race of North-western Europe. Blue or grey eyes are to be found, though very rarely, among Indians, but the place to look for them is on the west coast, and ancient sea traffic is the only possible explanation of their occurrence.

In India the Aryan theory rests upon a solid basis of sentiment. Indian *amour propre* is gratified by the idea that Indians are Aryans, so to say, of the elder line;

British, French, and German Aryans of the younger and till lately relatively uncivilised branch. Since very few Indians are aware of the facts set out in the previous chapter with regard to the racial affinities and ancient cultural contacts of the Dravidian race, it commonly appears to an Indian that to be regarded as a Dravidian rather than an Aryan is to be denied his kinship with the western European and relegated to an inferior category. This idea is, of course, groundless.

The probable date, and essential character, of the Aryan intrusion has recently been argued by Myres[1] in connection with the horse. "The horse had been hunted for food since palæolithic times, but there is no clear evidence even of its domestication, even as a milch animal, outside the high plateaux of Central Asia, until a comparatively late date." In Europe the Halstatt culture is "the first great regional culture which made systematic use of the horse for riding as well as for driving."

[1] "Cambridge Ancient History," Vol. I., pp. 106-7.

In Asia "the first positive record is in a Babylonian tablet of about 2100 B.C., where it is described as the 'ass from the east' or 'from the mountains,' and it was therefore still a recent acquisition among the ass-using folk west of the Zagros range. Its arrival here is commonly referred to that irruption of fresh peoples from Iran and beyond who founded the barbarian Kassite dynasty of Babylon about 1750 B.C., and as there is no reason to believe that the great plateau of Iran was even then in much better condition than now to support an indigenous pastoral civilisation, it is probable that this irruption originated further to the north-east, on the Sarmatian flat land, and that it is to be connected, in its significance, if not precisely in date, with the irruption of Aryan-speaking folk into India from the same northern reservoir," and with westward movements into Europe across the Dnieper and via Galicia into Bohemia, as well as via the Balkan Peninsula into Asia Minor.

The Aryans, then, must be regarded as

relatively barbaric invaders, provided by their horses with an immense advantage for rapid and concerted movement, and so for military and political mastery of peoples, who as in the cases of the Sumerians and Dravidians lacked this equipment for victory and power, in spite of their superiority in those elements of culture which make for wealth and civilisation, and whose very superiority in wealth was an enticement to the invaders. The latter no doubt brought other new culture elements into India besides the horse, among them, we have reason to believe, the practice of burning the dead, and associated ideas with regard to life after death, which mingled with Dravidian beliefs without superseding them. An old Greek myth discusses the relative merits of the equine and pre-equine cultures. Poseidon and Athena disputed as to which was entitled, by having conferred the more valuable gift, to give a name to the city known to us as Athens. Poseidon gave the horse, Athena the olive, and the jury of gods gave the verdict to Athena, because her gift was associated with peaceful industry, and that of Poseidon with war. If, on similar principles, we reckon Egyptian above Hykso culture, and that of the Romano-Greek Empire above that of the Turks who overthrew it, we should also esteem Dravidian culture above the Aryan at the time of the irruption.

Still more, it is necessary to approach with an open mind the question of the proportions in which the two elements entered into the make up of Indian civilisation as we know it. The analogy of the early history of Greece may be of some help; but to make the cases more closely parallel we must imagine what that history would have been if the barbarian invasions which presumably crushed the Minoan and Mycenæan cultures had never penetrated beyond the Gulf of Corinth, and the Peloponnesus had maintained its ancient language and traditions.

It is curious that for the most part even the foreign observers in India who have been struck with what may be termed the general racial homogeneity of the great majority of the people of India, and who have drawn the natural inference that Indians are, in the main, Dravidians by race, still tend to accept without scrutiny the popular doctrine that Indian culture, religion, and philosophy are of Aryan origin. Thus Mr C. F. Oldham, whose striking and valuable book "The Sun and the Serpent" is largely devoted to showing the importance of the Dravidian element in the populations of North India, yet assumes that Brahmanism is Aryan in origin, and regards the mention in Sanscrit literature of Brahmans in a position of dominance in any Nāga (Dravidian) state as an indication of its having been Aryanised. But there is less than no evidence of the superiority of the Brahman caste, or even of the caste system itself, being an Aryan institution. Max Müller ("Chips," Vol. II., p. 311) asks:—

"Does caste, as we find it in Manu, and at the present day, form a part of the most ancient religious teaching of the Vedas?

We can answer with an emphatic 'No!' There is no authority whatever in the hymns of the Veda for the complicated system of caste; no authority for the degraded position of the Sudras; there is no law to prohibit the different classes of the people from living together, from eating and drinking together; no law to prohibit the marriage of people belonging to different castes; no law to brand the offspring of such marriages with an indelible stigma . . . there is no trace in the Veda of the atrocities of Siva and Kali, nor of the licentiousness of Krishna, nor of the miraculous adventures of Vishnu. We find in it no law to sanction the blasphemous pretensions of a priesthood to divine honours, or the degradation of any human being to a state below the animals. There is no text to countenance laws which allow the marriage of children, and prohibit the marriage of child-widows; and the unhallowed rite of burning the widow with the corpse of her husband is both against the spirit and the letter of the Veda."

The caste system, the sanctity of the Brahman, the worship of Kali, of Siva and Vishnu, of Parvati the consort, and Subrahmaniam and Ganesa, the sons of Siva, and of Krishna, the last incarnation of Vishnu, these things are not mere alien and unimportant accretions to an Indian culture of Aryan and Vedic origin, they are of the innermost essence of Indian culture. If Kali and Siva and Vishnu are not Vedic deities, and certainly they are not, they can hardly be Aryan, and there seems no other possible alternative than to suppose they are Dravidian. And if caste is not an Aryan institution, is it Dravidian?

Here the question is a little more complicated. The theory generally accepted among Indians is that caste is an institution that arose among the Aryans after they had settled in India and had developed a more highly organised industrial life based on agriculture; and that its basis is economic; it provided a simple, but advantageous, division of labour, and the principle of hereditary occupations was the easiest and most natural way of providing technical instruction. And in support of the view that caste did originally arise in some such way as this, the fact may be cited that new castes are thus brought into being. Prof. Radhakamal Mukerjee gives an interesting example in "The Foundations of Indian Economics." The oil-pressers of Bengal were all one caste until the device came in of making a hole at the bottom of the mortar in which oil seeds are pressed. Then the oil-pressers who adopted the new device became a separate caste, socially inferior to the caste that continued to use the old method of baling out the oil and of mopping it up with a cloth.

European observers commonly hold that the origins of caste are political rather than economic. Laying, perhaps, too great emphasis on the social stratification of the caste system, and on the association of caste superiority with relatively fair colouration, they attribute the whole institution to a succession of invasions of

India by the passes of the North-west, the invaders being in each case fairer, physically bigger and more war-like than the previous inhabitants. Each fresh body of invaders spread itself over the country, and selected wives from the native young women, but, actuated by racial pride, imposed on their children, and especially on their daughters, a strict prohibition of any further intermarriage. Hence their descendants became an exclusive caste.

There are doubtless elements of truth in both these theories, but they require modification to suit the facts. On either theory North India rather than South India should be the special home of the caste system; for the first theory because it is more highly Aryanised, and for the second, because it is the part whose history has been most dominated by successive invasions. But notoriously the caste system is much stronger, much more elaborate, and plays a much larger part in social life in South India than in North India; and it reaches its highest development in that part of India which is most effectively cut off from land invasions from the north, the narrow strip of land between the Western Ghats and the Arabian Sea. This fact is by itself sufficient to prove that caste is of Dravidian rather than of Aryan origin. The question of the probable manner of its evolution will be dealt with later.

In the work previously referred to, "The Sun and the Serpent," Mr Oldham collects the passages in the Vedas and Sanscrit epics which throw light upon the civilisation of Dravidian India at the time of the Aryan invasion. That the Aryans themselves were then essentially nomadic pastoralists, though possibly not altogether unacquainted with agriculture, is undisputed; the Dravidians were probably in a much more advanced stage of civilisation. It is only necessary to reproduce some of Mr Oldham's quotations from the Rig-Veda, that being the most ancient, and therefore the source on which we can best rely as indicating conditions at the actual time of the invasion rather than later. We have :

" Indra shattered, for Divodasa, the hundred castles of Sambara."

" Indra, wielder of the thunderbolt, warring on behalf of Purukutsa, thou didst overthrow the seven cities; thou didst cut off, for Sudas, the wealth of Anhas."

" Benevolent to man, thou hast broken the cities of Pipru ; and protected Rijisvan in his battles with the Dasyus."

" Thou didst boldly sweep away the wealth of Sushna ; thou didst shatter his castles."

Castles, cities and wealth—these are sufficiently significant. " In addition," says Mr Oldham, " Sanscrit writings ascribe to the Dravidian Asuras 'Luxury, the use of magic, superior architectural skill, and ability to restore the dead to life.' "

We must not let the full significance of these facts escape. They imply in pre-Aryan Dravidian India the existence of a priest-magician class or caste, such as apparently did not exist among the Aryans,[1] but which is one of the most important features of Hinduism. It points directly to the conclusion that the Brahman caste itself, and its position of dominance over even the Kshattriya or warrior caste is a Dravidian institution. This conclusion is borne out by detailed evidence quoted by Mr Oldham, though he fails to draw the obvious inference.

He notes (p. 80) that Krishna is recorded as the special protector of Brahmans, and as making a practice of washing their feet. That Krishna was a dark-skinned non-Aryan is a tradition which Indian pictorial art has faithfully preserved ; he is always painted blue. And the story of his descent is that besides being an incarnation of Vishnu, he was the son of Vasudeva, who was the great-grandson of Āryaka, a Nāga chief. The word Nāga means Serpent, or,

[1] To what extent it is to be inferred from the Rig-Veda that among the Aryans sacrifices and religious ceremonies were the function of a special section, or whether they were performed generally by heads of families, is a matter of dispute among scholars.

applied to human beings, serpent-worshipper, and in Sanscrit Epic literature it replaces the terms Asura, Dasyu, Daitya and Dānava, as the ordinary term for the still unconquered Dravidians of North India.

Again (p. 78), " Balarāma, the elder brother of Krishna, is represented as having his head sheltered by the hoods of many serpents. He is said to have been an incarnation of Sesha Nāga, and at his death his soul, in the form of a great serpent, escaped from his mouth."

From the Mahābhārata we learn (p. 68) that " Sakra, the chief priest of the Asuras " (Dravidians), "divided himself by the power of asceticism and became the spiritual guide of both the Daityas " (Dravidians) " and the Dēvas " (Aryans). This obviously records the success of the priestly caste of the Dravidians in imposing their spiritual authority on the Aryans also.

The Vishnu Purana yields the information that one Usanas or Sakra lighted fires, said *mantras* and recited the Atharva Veda for the success of the Asuras, or Dravidians, against Indra, the god of the Aryans. He also restored to life Dravidian Dānavas, who had been killed by the Aryan Dēvas; so clearly he was a Dravidian priest-magician. He was a son of the great rishi Bhrigu, who therefore was presumably also a Dravidian priest-magician. But the sons of Bhrigu were Brahmans, and were the spiritual guides of the Daitya (Dravidian) chief Hiranyakasipu.

To this evidence, for which I am indebted to Mr Oldham, I must add two observations founded on familiar facts: (1) If the Brahmans had been originally an Aryan priestly caste, the worship of the Vedic deities, Varuna, Indra and the rest, would have become as dominant in Hindu religion as the Brahmans are in Hindu society. Actually their worship has, in spite of the continual influence of the religious use of the Vedas, practically disappeared, being replaced by that of non-Vedic deities; and (2) the distinguishing mark of the Brahman caste is the cord of cotton thread worn over one shoulder and under the opposite arm, which indicates an original association of the caste with cotton spinning, which certainly was no art of the Vedic Aryans.

The Aryan invasion may reasonably be regarded as one of the long series of exoduses of pastoral tribes from Asiatic steppes that have repeatedly devastated surrounding agricultural districts. The paradox is now established on a pretty solid basis of evidence that intensive agriculture among the first pioneers of progress preceded extensive agriculture, and that agriculture was practised before the pastoral stage was reached. But cattle and sheep having been domesticated by the agriculturists of Egypt and Mesopotamia, the breeding of such animals can hardly fail to have spread more rapidly among neighbouring hunting tribes than the more laborious art of cereal cultivation.[1] The change from the hunting to the pastoral life involves an immediate

[1] Similarly, though the steam-engine in England was first applied to mining, then to textile manufacture, and later to transport, in distant countries this order was reversed.

increase of births and decrease of deaths. A supply of milk for infants makes earlier weaning possible, together with a reduction of child mortality and a more vigorous growth. A supply of milk for the mother reduces the strain of child-bearing, prolongs the period of fertility, and, combined with a shortening of the duration of suckling after each birth, leads to a shortening of the intervals between successive births. For a limited number of generations the rapidly increasing population can be maintained by the same area of land, used as pasture, as had previously been required for much smaller numbers as hunting ground, but the time comes when the pasture grounds are fully exploited and still the population grows. Then something has to happen, and Hykso or Hun or Mogul or Turkish treks, great floods of conquering hordes overwhelming even powerful empires, are examples of what has happened. Where the pastoralists are horse-breeders these movements become most devastating. India, though relatively remote and difficult of access, has undergone such pastoralist invasions repeatedly; the Mogul invasion under Babur was the last, the Aryan invasion, led according to the Vedas by the god Indra, was the first; but there were many in between.

The Aryan descent into India was probably by the Khyber Pass, which gave entrance to the northern corner of the Punjab. The invaders probably found at first only thinly inhabited lands, on which they and their stock could increase and multiply. Later came the time of inter-racial conflict with Dravidians and pre-Dravidians which must have passed through three stages. The first, indicated by the Rig-Veda, was the stage of slaughter and devastation, the superior mobility of the invaders enabling them to concentrate an overwhelming force against each centre of resistance; Uritsa was devoured, Bāla was overthrown, the seven cities, the cities of Pipru were rased, the castles of Sushna were shattered, and his wealth became the booty of the worshippers of Indra. The second stage came with the realisation that has always come to such invaders sooner or later, that it was more profitable to enslave than to kill; and then Aryan kingdoms were established, guarded by an Aryan soldiery, and sustained by the labours of Dravidian peasants and artisans. Thirdly came the stage depicted in the Epics, when Aryan kingdoms warred and made alliances indiscriminately with one another and with the Dravidian states surrounding them that still maintained their independence.

During the second stage, and still more during the third, a mutual action and reaction was taking place. Intercourse included intermarriage; it involved a struggle for survival between languages. That the more brawny but thicker-witted Aryan should learn the extraordinarily difficult language of "the ill-speaking man," as the Vedas term the Dravidian, was not to be supposed. The Dravidian instead had to learn Sanscrit.

What happened then we can infer from

the experience of South India in recent times. In the eighteenth century, with the overthrow of Dupleix, the English East India Company became the ruling power in the Carnatic. Mastery of the English language became a means to profit, influence and power. The Brahman caste, habituated to an intellectual life, and trained in the exercise of verbal memory to an astonishing degree, found here an opportunity. At the present day, though there still remain in the Tamil country some "temple Brahmans" who are more familiar with Sanscrit than with English, with the Vedas than with Shakespeare, they are a very small minority of the caste. The ordinary Tamil Brahman speaks English more accurately than Tamil, writes it more easily and rapidly, reads it much more frequently, and has practically adopted English literature as his own; and, accordingly, the staffs both of Government offices and those of mercantile houses consist almost entirely of Brahmans, and they almost monopolise the legal and journalistic professions.

Similar motives existed from the time of the establishment of Aryan predominance in the Punjab to induce the Dravidian Brahmans of that and neighbouring districts to adopt Sanscrit as their language, and to constitute themselves the guardians and exponents of the Vedas. They had behind them the traditions of magic and of priest-craft, of which the underlying principle is the quest for any sort of recondite or esoteric learning that either tends to differentiate the sacred caste from the common people, or in any other way tends to the acquisition of power and influence. And the Brahmans having thus taken the initiative in spreading the use of Sanscrit, or Sanscrit derivatives, among the Dravidian population, others less eagerly and with greater difficulty followed by degrees, just as has happened with the spread of English in the Madras Presidency.

While the Dravidians were thus Aryanised in language, the Aryans were Dravidised in culture. What that meant is a question to be dealt with below. But one feature of the change must be mentioned here. They were brought under Brahman dominance. The immediate effect of the incursion into India of conquering tribes that had no specialised priestly caste, and of the period of fierce warfare that ensued, was to depose the priestly caste temporarily from its supremacy, and to make it yield precedence to the warrior caste. Not until many generations had passed, centuries during which the Indian environment had worked its effect, the terrific heat of the summer sun, the monsoon deluges, hurricanes, pestilences, famines, all combining to teach men to honour rather those who asserted their power to control the elements and conciliate angry deities than those who yielded the sword, did the Brahman caste succeed in re-establishing its primacy. To this deposition and restoration we have a later parallel in the history of the Mogul Empire ; and the nature of the social forces at work is also illustrated by the speedy domination of the descendants of Sivaji by their Brahman ministers. After Brahman ascendancy had been re-established, it may possibly be conjectured that the Brahman caste became largely Aryanised in blood, as the most powerful men were able to secure in marriage the fairest brides.

CHAPTER III

THE ANTIQUITY OF DRAVIDIAN CIVILISATION

THE circumstance which has made possible the belief that Sanscritic civilisation is more ancient than Dravidian, and that Indian culture has an Aryan and Sanscritic origin, rather than Dravidian, is the fact that South India cannot show either writings or buildings of incontestable antiquity. It by no means follows that South India did not possess them, for their complete disappearance is the natural consequence of the perishable nature of the materials used, and the destructive power of a hot, damp climate and superabundant insect life. Manuscripts are written on palm leaves. The most ancient temples cannot be accurately dated, but no one claims that they come either before or very

Plate II. Rock Tobb found in Cairn at Gazzalakonda, Kurnul, unopened

near the Christian era. But these earliest extant stone buildings (apart from dolmens and other rude stone monuments) unmistakably betray their indebtedness to a more ancient architectural art and tradition. Though built of hard granitic rock, a most intractable material, they display the utmost elaboration of ornament. This must have been worked up slowly through centuries by workers in more manageable materials, so that the earliest builders of temples and palaces of stone, instead of, as in other countries, first experimenting in simple forms, and gradually adding ornament to ornament, attempted from the beginning a height of elaboration never reached elsewhere in material of the same character. The result, as in the great temple of Siva and Menakshi at Madura, is vastly impressive ; disgusting and repellent to most European eyes, but magnificent and beautiful to most Indians. The whole story of Dravidian temple architecture can be read in a day at the ancient sacred city of Conjiveram, where may be seen one of the most ancient stone temples of South India in ruins; others, less ancient, but still venerable, in use and in good repair, others being rebuilt or extended at the cost of the Nattukottai Chetties; and in the paddy fields the sites of the temples of wood, long ago completely destroyed by the white ant, marked by the sacred emblems of Siva, the *lingams* of the hardest and most imperishable stone.

North India can boast, in the red sandstone and white marble tombs, palaces and mosques of the Mogul Emperors, and in the palaces of the Rajput princes, an architecture which Europeans regard as far more beautiful than anything that South India can show. But in the way of Hindu temples there is nothing in North India equal to the sumptuous greatness and elaboration of the great shrines of the South. Dravidian architecture in the deltaic lands of the Carnatic was unchecked in its continuous evolution up to the fall of the Vijayanagar Empire at Talakota in A.D. 1565, and even then the check was

PLATE III. ROCK TOBB FOUND IN CAIRN AT GAZZALAKONDA, KURNUL, OPENED

only temporary and partial. One of its most notable achievements, the palace of Tirumalai Naik at Madura, is of later date; and the curious city of Sivaganga, lying remote from the railway, the centre from which the Nattukottai Chetties send out the carefully trained young men who finance the rice trade of Burma, and who carry on banking operations far and wide in India and abroad, is also the central school of Dravidian architecture in the ancient tradition. There the maistries are trained under the eyes of their patrons, before they go out to other cities to build and restore the temples of Siva, a work to which the Chetties by caste tradition should devote one-tenth of the profits of their usury.

In spite of the absence of Dravidian architecture of anything approaching Vedic antiquity, the facts relating to it tend on the whole to point to a greater antiquity for Dravidian than for Aryan civilisation. Similarly with regard to literature. There is no extant Tamil literature, or literature in any other Dravidian language, to which a very high antiquity is assigned. But the very character of the Tamil language, the perfection with which it has been developed into an organ for precise and subtle thought, combined with the fact that it represents a much earlier stage in the evolution of inflexional language than any Indo-Germanic tongue, suggests, though of course it does not prove, the priority of the Dravidians in attaining settled order and regular government; just as the fact that the Greek language attained its perfection while still highly inflected, and the English language only after its inflections had almost all been lost, was a result of Greek priority in civilisation over ourselves. Here I may note that a most interesting task is waiting for some philologist well trained in both Indo-Germanic and Dravidian languages, in the investigation of the large number of words which are common to Tamil and Sanscrit. Those which can also be found in some other Indo-Germanic language may be presumed to be Tamil borrowings from Sanscrit; those that cannot, are presum-

Plate IV. Dolmen at Kalyandrug, Anartapur

ably Sanscrit borrowings from extinct Dravidian languages of North India. In this way definite information can be obtained with regard to the differences of culture between the two races when Aryan and Dravidian first came into contact. One philologist, who began on this enquiry without taking it very far, told me that words relating to the cultivation of flowers and the making of garlands belong to the latter group. The significance of this statement, if it can be confirmed, is obvious.

Very suggestive, again, are the Tamil calendars. There are two, an ecclesiastical calendar and a civil one. The ecclesiastical calendar, like other Asiatic calendars, including the Telugu calendar, is lunar, and does not call for special remark. But the civil calendar is solar, truly and completely solar, and is not, like ours, an originally lunar calendar modified to fit the solar year. It is so uncompromisingly solar that it does not even concern itself to make a month consist of so many days. The ecliptic is divided into twelve divisions, and at whatever moment in the morning, noon or night, the sun enters a new division, at that moment the new month begins. Days begin at sunrise, not the local time of sunrise for any place in India, but at the calculated moment of sunrise at the spot on the equator which is also on the meridian of the site of the ancient Tamil observatory. I do not know whether anyone has ever assigned a date to the adoption of this unique calendar. That it is unique, and that it aims at a degree of astronomical accuracy and consistency beyond that of any other calendar in use, even at the sacrifice of some practical convenience, is very significant. It proves the independence and continuous activity of Dravidian science in the part of India least exposed to non-Dravidian influences.

So far, apart from references to Dravidian cities and Dravidian arts in the Vedas, nothing has been cited which can be regarded as a proof of the antiquity of Dravidian culture. Proofs, however, in abundance, of the extreme antiquity of intercourse by sea between South India and other centres of civilisation, may be found in the published researches of G. Elliot Smith, Wilfred H. Schoff, J. Wilfrid Jackson, W. J. Perry and others, whose results are conveniently summed up for the general reader by Mr Perry in his "Children of the Sun." Here I propose to add a few only which have come to my knowledge through other channels.

(1) Logan, in his classic, "District Manual of Malabar," gives an account of the language of the island of Minicoy, which lies between the west coast of India and the Laccadive Islands, and records the curious fact that the islanders have a duodecimal system of notation, up to 100. The cardinal numbers are as follows:

1 ēkkē, 2 dē, 3 tinē, 4 hattari, 5 pahē, 6 hayē, 7 hatti, 8 areg, 9 nuvē, 10 dihē, 11 egārā eklus, 12 dolōss, 13 dolōss ēkkē, 14 dolōss dē, and so on to 23 dolōss eklus, 24 phasihi, 25 phasihi ēkkē, 36 tintolōss, 48 phanass, 60 phattolōss, 72 phahitti, 84 haidolōss, 96 hiyā, 100 hiyā hattari or

sattikā, 101 sattikā ēkkē, 200 dē sattikā, etc.

The word for 100 is derived from the mainland, and represents a disharmonic intrusion into the duodecimal system. But what about the origin of the system itself? It may be said that for us the establishment of such a system represents an unattainable mathematical ideal. Certainly the islanders of Minicoy could not have evolved it for themselves, nor could they have obtained it from India. The nearest possible source is Mesopotamia; but whether the precise words used for the different numbers confirm or cast doubt upon a Sumerian or Chaldæan origin I am unable to say.

(2) That India is rich in dolmens, kistvæns, cairns and similar remains proving the influence of the seafarers who carried far and wide the "heliolithic culture" is a very familiar fact. Not so familiar is the fact that the explorations of the Hyderabad Archæological Society into Hyderabad cairns have brought to light pottery with incised marks, the majority of which are

identical with symbols found by Sir Arthur Evans to have been in use in Minoan Crete.

(3) Shortly before the outbreak of the war there were found at Adichanallur in the Tinnevelly District, *i.e.* at the extreme south of India, remains which are on view in the Madras Museum. They consisted of large earthenware pots, used for burial, skeletons[1] in a doubled-up position being found inside, and with them bronze figures of a variety of domestic animals. The most lifelike of all is one of a pariah dog. By far the most numerous are figures of buffaloes; and it is a striking fact that there is not a single representation of the ox. The natural inference is that these remains date from a period before the introduction of oxen, but after the successful domestication of the buffalo. The wild ox of India (bison or gaur) never has been domesticated, and though the origin of the Indian domesticated ox is unknown, it pretty certainly came from some place outside India. Among the Adichanallur finds there are fillets of gold

[1] See Note at end of Chapter.

beaten very thin, evidently made to be worn on the foreheads of priests, and in all respects similar to those discovered in Minoan Crete ; and a bronze figure which can only be described as apparently that of a woman in Eskimo costume.

That either these gold fillets or the incised marks on the pottery in the Hyderabad cairns should be attributed to a direct contact between the seafarers who had their capital at Knossos and the pre-Aryan Dravidians is not probable, as while the Minoans preceded the Phœnicians in the exploration of the shores of the Mediterranean, and perhaps of the Atlantic, including even our own coasts, there is, so far as I know, no evidence that they were also the pioneers in the Red Sea, or the Persian Gulf, or the Indian Ocean. Rather it would appear probable that Minoan exploration westwards and Phœnician exploration eastwards and southwards started at approximately the same time, in consequence, we may imagine, of improvements in the arts of shipbuilding

PLATE V. BRONZE STATUETTE, ADICHANALLUR

and navigation, which might have been due neither to Minoan nor Phœnician invention, but to the Egyptians. Probably the letter signs on the Hyderabad cairn pottery were Phœnician as well as Minoan; and Phœnician priests used similar gold fillets.

Dravidian art also bears signs of some direct or indirect connection with that of Knossos. Deities, whether male like Siva, or female like Kali, are represented as having unnaturally exaggerated waists, without any constricting agency being indicated. In Minoan art waists are even smaller, but men and women are represented as wearing metal girdles which would almost seem to have been put on in childhood and never taken off. It would appear that although the practice of confining the waist did not spread to India, an artistic convention based upon that practice did get established there.

I am too little acquainted with Indian folklore to be able to present more than specimens of the evidence from that source. The story of Manu and the flood, and the ark carrying Manu and seven wise men and all manners of seeds, is obviously a variant of the Babylonian tradition of the Deluge. The story of the Churning of the Ocean points most unmistakably to ancient Dravidian commerce and its character. The gods churned the ocean in order to obtain the nectar Amrit; to supply the implement the Snake God, Ananda, tore up the rock Mandara. The significance of his intervention will be seen from Chapter IV. By the churning the gods obtained, first gums, then various essences, then gold, then wine, then the white steed, then the jewel Kaustubha, and at last the longed-for nectar, brought in a white vessel. Men got a taste of the nectar, and there ensued a long and desperate battle between the gods and the men for the possession of the white vessel, but finally the gods were victorious, and carried it off in triumph to the mountains. All these details are suggestive, but we are specially intrigued by the question

> "That nectar, was it beer or whisky-toddy?
> Some think the Gaelic mixture, *I* the Saxon."

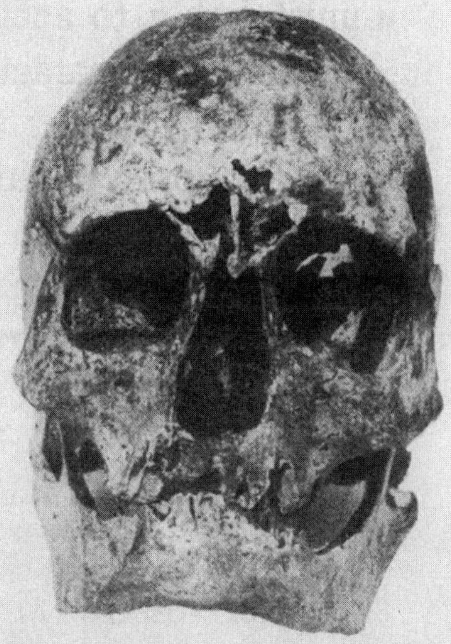

PLATE VI. ADICHANALLUR SKULL, FRONT VIEW

Calverley's jest takes on a serious meaning, for the two obvious answers are—(1) that the nectar Amrit was Egyptian beer, and (2) that it was, not whisky-toddy, but true toddy, the fermented juice collected from the cut fronds of the date palm, palmyra, or coco-nut palm, which is the great intoxicating beverage of India, stronger than our beer, with an average content of about 8 per cent. of alcohol, and that the art of making toddy reached India by sea from Mesopotamia, the home of date-palm cultivation.

Between four and five thousand years ago Dravidian India received the seeds of many sorts of culture by sea from Egypt, or from Mesopotamia, or more probably from both, and received them into fertile soil. When carried into lands inhabited by less gifted races these cultures became fossilised and underwent chiefly degenerative changes, as shown by Perry in "The Children of the Sun," but in India they became the starting-point of a new development, pushed forward by the native genius of the

Dravidian race, and evolving in harmony with the Indian geographical environment.

The following conclusions then appear to be indicated by the evidence cited:

(1) That there was in India at the time of the Aryan invasions a Dravidian civilisation of a more elaborate and developed character than the civilisation, if civilisation it can be called, of the Aryans.

(2) That in so far as this Dravidian civilisation was derived from outside sources its origin is to be traced to Egypt and Mesopotamia, linked up with India by sea commerce.

(3) That Dravidian civilisation resembled that of Egypt and Mesopotamia in the importance of the influence exerted in its evolution by religious ideas, and in the dominance of a priestly class or caste.

(4) That the first step towards the linking up of India with Egypt was accomplished when the Egyptians navigated the Red Sea, and reached the Land of Punt. The Dravidians themselves were early navigators, though on a more modest scale, and, as

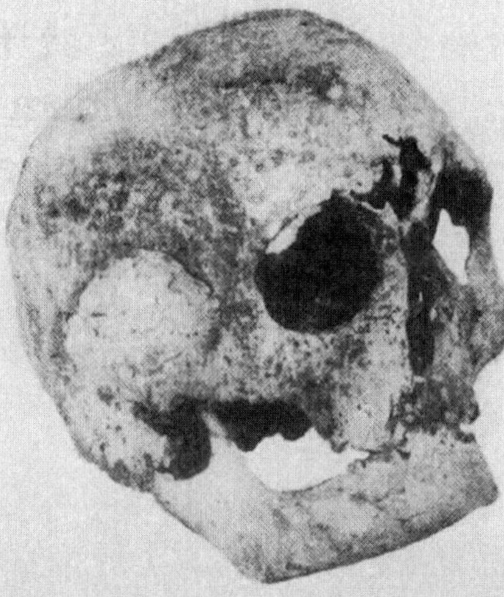

PLATE VII. ADICHANALLUR SKULL, SIDE VIEW

Elliot Smith has shown, their earliest boats were copied from Egyptian models. In this connection it should be noticed that the long chain of backwaters on the West Coast supply a sort of elementary school of navigation, and the steady wind from the shore during the period of the North-east monsoon is a strong encouragement to those who have learnt their first lessons in those backwaters to proceed to the second adventure on the open sea, which is further stimulated by the great abundance of excellent fish on that coast. It is notable that the people of Africa, apart from the Egyptians, never invented ships, though on parts of the coast there are inducements similar to those on the Indian coast.

[NOTE.—Prof. Elliot Smith writes:—"I have examined two skulls from Adichanallur. One was quite indistinguishable from the early Egyptian type. The other, though not so typical, comes well within the range of variation of that type." The skull in the illustrations is a third.]

CHAPTER IV

THE EVOLUTION OF INDIAN RELIGIOUS IDEAS

PERSISTENT attempts have been made to relate Hindu religion as it is to the deities hymned in the Vedas, but without success. Not only is it impossible to identify Indra with Vishnu or Siva, impossible to find Kali in the Vedas or the Maruts in modern Hinduism, but Vedic hymns and Hindu religion are expressions of two very different attitudes of mind. The Vedas display a childlike attitude of mind, a straightforward deification of the most impressive natural phenomena, and the adoption of one of the resulting deities as a tribal god. Hinduism shows a philosophic bent of mind, a continuous search after an ever more satisfactory explanation of the universe. In the existing deities and worship of South India we can trace that development, because, just as the sands of Egypt have the virtue of safeguarding and preserving material remains of the past, the Dravidian mind and social life has the characteristic of retaining and handing on from generation to generation whatever acquisitions it makes in ideas or customs, refusing to discard the old when it adopts the new.

Among the most ancient elements of Indian religion we may place the worship of the cobra, the "good snake." All over India cobras are exceedingly abundant, and Indian folk-lore is full of stories in which the cobra deity plays a benevolent part. That cobra worship was dominant among the Dravidians in the Vedic period is shown by the term Nāga gradually superseding the other names used in Sanscrit literature for the Dravidians. Mr Oldham points out that a close connection between Buddhism and Cobra worship is shown by Fergusson's photographs of the Amrāvati sculptures ("The Sun and the Serpent,"

p. 178), and that "in 1898 the stupas erected over the relics of the Sakyas, who were killed when Kapiladavastu was destroyed by the King of Magadha, were opened and in nearly every relic was found the representation of a Nāga. One of these caskets, which contained a golden Nāga, bore the name of Mahānāman, one of Buddha's own family, who succeeded to the throne which would have been inherited by Gautama himself had he not renounced the world."

Seeing how emphatically the cobra is an Indian snake, and remembering that much the larger part of the deaths in India attributable to wild animals are due to snake bite, and that among Indian snakes the cobra is pre-eminent, it is rather curious that Mr Oldham thinks the Dravidians brought snake worship with them into India from Persia or the Persian borders, and Prof. Elliot Smith and Mr Perry think that it came to India from Egypt, all rejecting the idea that it originated in India itself. But the range of the cobra both in Africa and Western Asia is wide, and in early days the numbers of cobras outside India probably much greater than now, and the sacred uræus of the Egyptians was a cobra, hence the balance of probability appears to be in favour of the Egyptian origin of this feature of Indian religion. If we admit the theory that the idea of worshipping one particular species of snake was introduced into India from outside, at any rate the Indian mind was well prepared, by first hand acquaintance with the reptile to be deified, to receive that idea into a fertile soil.

One of the most progressive and highly educated castes of South India is that of the Nayars or Nairs of the west coast. A very interesting experience to me was a call upon a Nayar family of Trichur with Mr Anandakrishna Aiyar, then State Anthropologist of Cochin and curator of the State museum and zoological gardens. We were received very gracefully by a young lady who could converse intelligently in English and French, and who had musical accomplishments. A younger brother, a bright boy of twelve, was studying Algebra with a tutor. Later we went round the back of the house into the garden where, overgrown by trees and bushes, was the cobra shrine. It was a group of granite blocks, with cobras erect with distended hoods carved on them, enclosed by railings, and, probably, living cobras close by, though we did not see them. To that shrine a Nambudiri Brahman must come periodically, and do *pujah* to the cobras, lest they bite the Nayars.

A deity possibly older even than the Cobra, and a deity who appears to be purely Dravidian, is Muniswami. The suggested interpretation of the name is "the angry deity." He is a malignant spirit who haunts certain trees and houses, and who betrays his presence in a tree by the fall of a branch to the injury or danger of someone below, and his presence in a house by calamities to the inhabitants. When his presence is either known or suspected prudence dictates propitiation. In the case of a tree this is accomplished by the nightly burning of little native oil lamps, and occasional offerings of fruit and flowers; in the case of a house an annual *pujah* must be celebrated. Muniswami is much in evidence all over South India, and in Madras, with a Puck-like stroke of humour, he selected among his various haunts a tree in the compound of the museum, and another in that of the house of the Anglican Bishop, and beneath these two trees lights burned, and probably still burn, in despite of Western science and Protestant Christianity.

Muniswami's activities as a haunter of houses were brought to my notice by my being asked to contribute to the cost of an annual Muniswami *pujah* on behalf of a house that originally had been the official residence of the Commander-in-Chief, and which, after having been put to various uses, had been allotted to offices for various small governmental departments. I asked what evidence there was that Muniswami haunted the house, what had he ever done?

The answer was that up to date he had done nothing of note, but that there was ample evidence to prove the general proposition that once an annual *pujah* to Muniswami was instituted in any house, he speedily got to count on it and got very angry if it was ever omitted. A terrible example from Ootacamund was quoted, in the case of a house that passed out of Indian into European ownership. The new owner dropped the *pujah*, and immediately a series of dire calamities befel him and his family, till he was convinced of the necessity of re-instituting it. Accordingly I added my contribution to the collection, and one Sunday night, a sheep and a supply of arrack having been bought, the deity was duly honoured and feasted to his entire satisfaction, and when he had had his fill of meat and drink, the worshippers finished up what remained. Muniswami, I was told, has a generous side to his character, he likes his worshippers to enjoy themselves.

Assuming, provisionally, that snake worship was not indigenous to India, but was brought there from its original home in Egypt, what connection, if any, is there between cobra worship and Muniswami ?

The answer to this question obviously depends on the working of the Dravidian mind. Now I think all who have had experience in teaching in South India will agree with my observation, that the outstanding quality of the Dravidian [1] mind is a propensity, which almost appears to be a craving, to generalise, to reach as quickly as possible some broad general principle, from which to make subsequent deductions ; and the associated defects accompanying this quality are, firstly, undue haste in forming generalisations on insufficient evidence and excessive reluctance to discard any generalisation after it has been formed in the mind. The earliest evidence we have with regard to cobra worship shows it as an organised cult, the state worship, or part of the state worship of petty kings who called themselves, and were called, Nāgas

[1] For the sociological explanation of the pre-eminence of the Dravidian mind in this characteristic see Chapter V.

or Cobras. This fact is quite in harmony with the theory that the cult was introduced by strangers who acquired power and authority by bringing new arts and knowledge. But because the cobra is what it is in India, the priestly and state cult became also a popular one. And with the acceptance of cobra worship came also the acceptance of the general principle that what is feared should also be worshipped.

The same idea, combined with the idea that that from which benefit is expected should also be worshipped, apparently underlies the annual festival of Ayuda Pujah. On that day every craftsman worships the instruments of his craft. The university student worships his textbooks, his lecture notes, and his fountain pen, the coachman his employer's carriage, the chauffeur his employer's motor-car, the factory operatives—if permitted—worship the machinery, sacrificing sheep, and, as a disgusted manager remarked to me, "making a beastly mess." Less awe-inspiring things get smaller offerings; a few sticks of incense and a smear of red paint was considered enough to propitiate the deity residing in my motor-bicycle, a colleague's victoria was allowed offerings of fruit and lighted lamps, placed at sunset in front of each wheel. That, the coachman told me, was sufficient to prevent the spirit of the carriage from contriving an accident for those who used it during the ensuing twelve months.

From these cruder conceptions Dravidian thought passed on to the conception of a deity at once lavish and terrible, fickle and incomprehensible, and therefore female, from whom comes small-pox, cholera, and famine, but also rich harvests. She is the Village Goddess, and bears innumerable names, the commonest perhaps being Gangamma in Telugu villages and Mariyamman or Mariyattal in Tamil villages.[1] Her characteristics are so similar that we can hardly refrain from identifying her

[1] See the most interesting book on "Village Deities of South India," by Bishop Whitehead of Madras.

with Kali, Kali with the rounded limbs, wide hips, swelling breasts, exaggerated waist, and with many arms brandishing deadly weapons, tirelessly dancing, a fit emblem indeed for Nature as she is in India, so bountiful in her kindly moods, so deadly when the whim takes her. In some villages the Village Goddess is worshipped regularly or periodically, once a year, or once in twelve years ; in other places only when she shows signs of anger, as by repeated failure of the rains, or by pestilence. She rejoices in blood, and demands wholesale sacrifice of male animals, cocks, rams, he-goats, but most of all the male buffalo.

In the Telugu country Gangamma has no rival in the esteem of the villagers. But I am told on good authority that psychological necessities have produced a change in the feeling of her worshippers that is not yet apparent in the manner of the worship. That change may only have taken place since British government established peace and order, and thereby made possible the optimistic view that " God's in his heaven, all's right with the world." The change alleged is that the Telugu villager loves rather than fears Gangamma, and regards her rather as the power that wards off pestilence and puts a period to drought, than as the sender of these calamities.

The same psychological need, the need of a benevolent and protective deity, has from distant ages past been met in the Tamil country by the god Aiyanar. He is the village god, as Gangamma and her sisters are the village goddesses. Usually he demands no blood sacrifices; but recently when the cotton operatives of Madura came out on strike and swore to Aiyanar that they would not return to work until the whole of their demands had been conceded, and actually went back on a favourable compromise, a sheep had to be sacrificed to Aiyanar to atone for the broken vow.

Every night Aiyanar rides round the village to protect it from ghostly dangers. Well-to-do villages provide Aiyanar with a miniature temple to live in, usually placed on the top of any available knoll or hillock from which as extended a view as possible can be obtained. On a platform outside are placed two horses, of the size and general build of Shire stallions, built of brick and mortar, covered with plaster, gaily caparisoned, and each with a diminutive statue of an attendant groom, holding the horse ready for Aiyanar to mount. In the city of Kumbakonam the chief temple of Aiyanar has a horse and elephant instead of two horses, but this is the only example of that variant which I have seen. Villages which have not made the necessary effort to provide so fully for Aiyanar's requirements give him a habitation in the open air under trees, and expect him to do his best with hollow horses of terra-cotta, very rudely fashioned. In this case a new one is made for him every year, and so he accumulates a considerable stud, but of very sorry steeds, some lacking tails, many without heads, and very few with four legs.

The foregoing cults all belong to the first period in the history of Dravidian religious thought, the period before the momentous discovery was made of the biological facts relating to paternity. How difficult it was to make that discovery independently, and what a weird variety of hypothetical explanations of the birth of children have been accepted in the process of searching for the truth, has been shown by Mr E. S. Hartland in "Primitive Paternity." Once the knowledge of the truth was reached in the early centres of civilisation it spread fairly quickly nearly all over the world, and hence is known at the present day to innumerable tribes in a very low stage of culture. But in the beginning a very high stage had to be reached to make the first discovery possible. Assuming, as we may with confidence, that observations on domestic animals first gave the clue, and that even then there was a reluctance to make the inference that the same biological law applied to humanity, we must conclude that those nations that made the discovery must previously have supplemented hunting by agriculture, then developed agriculture into their main means of subsistence, and brought in the ox to aid human muscle, and also have attained an economic surplus sufficient to give some of their number sufficient leisure for continued thought.

India appears to have been one of the few countries in which this discovery was made independently. A very high standard of intellectual culture was reached previously; and when the discovery was made, the wonderful nature of the truth made in India a deeper impression on the mind, and on the form of religion, than in any other part of the world.

To this day, as Messrs Spencer and Gillen discovered, many tribes of Australian natives hold that conception and birth are due to the action of spirits which haunt certain secluded spots, and seize opportunities when presented of entering the bodies of women, particularly of those who are young and plump, and so securing incarnation. The opinions which arose in India were naturally, in view of the higher mentality of the people, more varied; but the organised thought of the leisured priestly caste fastened upon the same idea as that still prevailing in the Australian bush, and developed it into a logical system. Birth being due to the entry of a spirit into the body of a woman, whence did that spirit come? Obviously out of some previous body, now dead. Hence by degrees is developed the idea of the transmigration of souls. Rejected theories, associating the phenomena of birth with animals and plants, yet leave their traces in the working out of the transmigration theory, which finally recognises unity and continuity throughout all organic life, and also the idea of progress, so that normally a soul in its series of incarnations gradually works up from the lowliest to the highest forms of life.

The doctrine of transmigration is supplemented by the doctrine of Karma, the two together making a complete philosophical system, which is as fundamental to Hinduism as to Buddhism and Jainism. The doctrine of Karma is the doctrine of moral causation, according to which every action during the period of any incarnation has its inevitable consequences, happiness resulting from virtue, and suffering from vice, if not during that life, at any rate in succeeding ones.

Though the original germ out of which the doctrines of Transmigration and Karma have grown was nothing but a delusion, they were too satisfying to the human intellect to be discarded when the original mistake was corrected. As soon as some sort of law and justice is atained in human society, the mind of man craves for an assurance that they are found, but in a much more perfect form, in the governance of the universe. Transmigration and Karma satisfy that craving more completely than does the Protestant doctrine of Heaven and Hell, or even the Catholic doctrine of Heaven, Hell and Purgatory. How easy would have been the task of Job's unpleasant "comforters" if they could have resorted to it! "My dear Job, it is quite true that during your present life you have been a model of respectability, but, obviously, in your last previous incarnation you must have been a shocking bad hat, and, no doubt, were cut short in the midst of your sins, so that you have a lot to pay for now. But cheer up! The hotter you are getting it now, the sooner those past sins will be wiped out, and in your next life you will reap the full reward of your virtue in this one."

The doctrine of Karma is doubtless valuable in assisting a man to bear his own misfortunes with equanimity, but to the outsider its effect in enabling him to look complacently on the sufferings of others is even more marked. Politically it is an anti-democratic force, as it tends to blunt indignation and nullify protests against social injustice. What valid objection is there to the privileged position of the Brahman and to the social degradation of the Paraiyan or Chandala, if the Brahman was born a Brahman because of his previous virtue, and the Paraiyan a Paraiyan either by way of promotion from a non-human existence, or as a penalty for sins committed as a member of a higher caste ? If, moreover, the virtuous Paraiyan will be born again in due time as a Brahman and the unworthy Brahman as a Paraiyan ?

Another consequence of the doctrine of Karma is that Indian ethics in relation to lower animals are the reverse of British. To the Indian the killing of animals, however quickly and painlessly, is a crime of the nature of murder ; to permit them to drag out a miserable existence, slowly dying of disease or starvation, is commendable, if they cannot be cured or fed ; and even the infliction of torture is scarcely regarded as being a wrong to the animal tortured, but only as an evil thing because tending to blunt the sensibilities of those who inflict or connive at it. Thus, for example, a general strike took place a few years ago in Bombay as a protest against the proposal of the municipality to establish a lethal chamber for dogs ; and, on the other hand, a strike of dhobies defeated the efforts of the Kodaikanal municipality to put a stop to cruelty to donkeys. In consequence, rats and mice and all sorts of vermin enjoy a peculiar immunity from human attempts on their lives; on the other hand, horses and draught oxen are probably treated worse than in any other civilised country. The reason is, of course, that if a rat be prematurely killed, the soul in it will be interrupted in its upward progress, failing to get the full experience and education of the rat stage, and, in consequence, will probably have to be reincarnated in a rat a second time, before passing on to the next rung in the ladder. On the other hand, additional suffering imposed on a horse or an ox will be credited to the account of the soul incarnated in the animal, and so will help its upward progress.

Though these ideas are common to Hinduism, Buddhism and Jainism, it is the Jains who are most thoroughgoing in their application. Jainism is a religious movement roughly contemporary with Buddhism, and while Buddhism is practically non-existent in India proper, the Jains numbered about a million and a quarter in the census of 1911, and by reason of greater average wealth and higher education, are of more than proportionate importance. Recently a leopard having been taken alive in the neighbourhood of Ajmere, the local Jains clubbed together in order to buy it, and then set it free. By saving its life they acquired merit. It is well known that the Buddhist Emperor Asoka established hospitals for animals as well as men; it is not so well known that such hospitals, called pinjrapoles, are still maintained by private benevolence in Madras and other places in South India. What is most remarkable is, that where maintained by Jains they have, at least in some instances, "jivat-khanas," or wards for sick insects. I cannot say how they are managed or administered. In Jainism, as in Buddhism, we may see a sublimation of the philosophy common to these religions and to Hinduism, by the infusion into them of a spirit of ethical earnestness, which endeavours to stimulate the votary to help other souls on their upward march, by holding out the hope that "merit" is thereby attained. The best result within the bounds of the Indian Empire is the admirable parochial priesthood system of Burma. To the work and influence of those celibate parish priests we must attribute the relatively high standard of elementary education of Burma, and the peculiar gentleness and amenity of Burmese village life.

The discovery of the biological fact of human paternity created the new gods Siva and Vishnu. Probably these two are only local variants of the same deity. Certainly outside India Vishnu is generally described as the deity of creation and preservation, and Siva as the deity of destruction; and, when Vishnu and Siva are linked together with Brahma to form the Hindu trinity (Trimurti), that is the division of functions between them. But primarily Siva is not the god of destruction, but of procreation, and his symbol is the lingam, the image of the male organ of reproduction, and therefore the symbol of life. In temples, and outside temples, and even apart from temples, the stone lingam is set up and worshipped, and one important caste in South India, the Lingayats, wear miniature lingams suspended from their necks. The Indian feeling on the subject is well illustrated by a legend commemorated in a carving in the temple of Siva and Menakshi at Madura. An old and virtuous couple who had long prayed in vain for a son, were told at last by the gods that their prayer would be granted, but in an unsatisfactory manner. They might, at their choice, have a son who should be worthless and dissolute, but who should survive them, and perform the ceremonies that would save them from the penalties inflicted on the souls of those who die childless, or they might have a beautiful and virtuous son who would die before them on reaching manhood. They chose the latter. The virtuous youth devoted himself to the worship of Siva, and when Death came to claim him, he clung so fast to the lingam that the god of the underworld could not tear him away, and he lived to be a blessing to his parents till the day of their death.

Similarly Vishnu, who is, like Siva, primarily the god of procreation, whose sign of the *nāmān*, the symbol of the act of coition, is marked with white and red paste on the foreheads of his male worshippers, is also, like Siva, secondarily the god of destruction. This is well illustrated by the chief sacred book of the Vaishnavites, the Bhagavat Gita—the Song of the Lord. Vishnu, incarnated as Krishna, is the charioteer of Arjuna in the great battle of Kurukshetra between the Kurus and Pandavas, who, though opposed, are yet kinsmen. Arjuna shrinks from entering into the fratricidal conflict. He appeals for advice to Krishna. Is it not a sin to kill kinsmen ? Does not such destruction lead to general lawlessness, to corruption of women, to confusion of caste, to neglect of religious ceremonies, and that to hell for those on behalf of whom the neglected ceremonies should have been performed ? Would it not be better to submit to be killed by the opposing faction without resistance? Krishna replies that it is Arjuna's duty to fight and be victorious; and in the argument expounds the Vaishnavite philosophy, and his own nature: "all-devouring Death am I, and the origin of all to come." Krishna is transfigured before Arjuna, who sees him in all the splendour of his divine form "with many mouths and eyes, with many divine ornaments, with many upraised divine weapons, all-marvellous, boundless, with face turned everywhere, his glory like that of a thousand suns blazing together in the sky." Arjuna exclaims, *inter alia*, "Like Time's destroying flames I see thy teeth; all the noblest warriors of our hosts hurrying rush into thy gaping mouths; some caught within the gaps between thy teeth, their heads crushed and ground to powder. All-swallowing, fiery-tongued, thou lickest up mankind, devouring all."

If Vishnu and Siva be local variants of the same deity, Vishnu must be attributed to a more northerly, Siva to a more southerly part of India. As remarked before, neither is a Vedic deity. But it is possible on the other hand that neither is purely Dravidian, though it is worthy of note that both Sankarachariya, the great apostle of the Saivites, and Ramanuja, the great apostle of the Vaishnavites, were natives of Dravidian India. It is, I think, a reasonable hypothesis that both Siva and Vishnu, though indigenous to India, and offspring of the Dravidian mind, are post-Vedic, and owe their origin in part to circumstances connected with the Aryan invasion.

The ground for this view is that Siva is closely connected with the bull, as Kali with the buffalo. As remarked above, the Indian domestic ox is pretty certainly derived from some non-Indian species of wild ox; and it is therefore natural to suppose that it was introduced by some invading pastoral tribes, by the Aryans, in fact. Further, this supposition explains very naturally the prohibition of beef-eating, and especially of cow-killing, which is so important a factor in Indian religion. The newcomers, in order to protect their cattle, would naturally make the killing of them, and especially the killing of cows, both a crime and a sin; and in order that the taboo might be effective, they would make the prohibition apply to their own people as well as to the natives. Vishnu, as well as Siva, is associated with the bull, one of the names of Krishna being Raja-gopala, the king-cowherd. Putting these indications together we reach the hypothetical conclusion that though the Dravidians in pre-Vedic times kept buffaloes, and used them in the cultivation of their paddy-fields, and therefore associated them with the Goddess of Fertility, they did not, in the proper sense of the word, breed them, and never learnt from them the biology of the birth of calves; but this knowledge came to them first by observation of the more valued bull and cow.

On the other hand, the fact that the Rig-Veda refers to phallic worship with disapproval seems to point to the establishment of the worship of Vishnu and Siva among the Dravidians before the Vedic period. And, as Prof. Elliot Smith reminds me, the original form of the Mother Goddess in Egypt was the Divine Cow, and that her worship was of extreme importance in Egypt from the fourth millennium onwards; and the Divine Bull was also of no small importance. Hence there is much to be said for the alternative hypothesis that the association of Siva with the bull, and the doctrine of the sacredness of the cow, were fully established in India, as a result of Egyptian contact, in pre-Aryan times.

Brahma is much less a popular deity than Vishnu or Siva; except as associated with Vishnu and Siva in the Trimurti, and as a name for the Universal Spirit in the pantheism of later Indian thought, he counts for little in South India. His one great shrine is in Rajputana, at Pushkar, near Ajmere. Like Vishnu and Siva, he is no Vedic deity; but the obvious connection between "Brahma" the god and "Brahman" the caste suggests that he belongs to the pre-Vedic period. If we accept Mr Oldham's conclusions in "The

Sun and the Serpent," that both the Solar and Lunar lines of Rajput princes are of Nāga or Dravidian origin, supported as they are by Elliot Smith's evidences of the wide diffusion of associated sun and serpent worship eastwards from Egypt, we may well see in Brahma the Sun God so imported into India.

Vishnu and Siva demand no blood sacrifices; but, in accordance with their character, they demand a maiden tribute. Little girls are recruited in various ways, some of them horrible, to be trained to serve the god as *devadasis*. In South India the more sacred a city is, the more rife venereal disease. In 1917 I was asked by the Government of Madras to investigate the accuracy of the vital statistics of the city of Kumbakonam. For many years an exceptionally low birth-rate oscillating above and below 30 per thousand had been recorded, and the Secretariate was convinced that a large proportion of the actual births escaped registration. The municipal council strenuously denied this, and the Collector of the district, after a special investigation, supported the municipality. When I reached the city I asked the municipal officials, "Why is the birth-rate low?" and was immediately answered, "There are twelve great temples and they all have Devadasis." In the hospital I found that exactly half the in-patients were exceptionally severe cases of gonorrhœa or syphilis, ordinary cases being treated by Ayurvedic physicians; one young Brahman assured me that four-fifths of the Brahman ladies were affected with these diseases. The doctor who had recently retired after thirty years' service as surgeon-in-charge of the hospital and the out-patients' department confirmed this estimate, but expressed the opinion that things were even worse among the Sourashtras, among whom, he said, the men were equally immoral, but knew less how to take care of themselves.

I can only refer very briefly to later and further developments of Indian religious thought. A Sun God, as sun worshippers have invariably thought, must necessarily have a consort, though the choice with some of them has fallen on the Moon Goddess, of others on the Earth Goddess. Sarasvati, the consort of Brahma, goddess of wisdom, and dweller, with Brahma, in the sky, would appear to be a moon goddess. Similarly, a god of procreation is naturally associated with a goddess of fertility, Vishnu with Lakshmi, Siva with Parvati. The Saivite myth of creation is simple and philosophical. For twelve years Siva and Parvati toiled at the task of fashioning plants and animals, and found it an uphill task. Then Siva bethought himself, and out of his right and left thighs respectively he made a male and a female Cupid, to inspire males and females with amorous passion, and thenceforward the work went on easily and irresistibly. There is a tendency to mate Siva with the old goddess Kali, Durga, etc., instead of allowing him his proper spouse. The great annual festival of Madura, in the extreme south, is an attempt, repeated every year, to accomplish the marriage of Siva to Menakshi. They live together in the great temple, and each spring Menakshi's brother is summoned from his home in a neighbouring village to solemnise the marriage. He comes, but as he crosses the dry bed of the River Vaigai every year an inauspicious sneeze from his cortège compels him to return, and the wedding is again postponed for twelve months. Menakshi is doubtless the local variant of the ordinary Dravidian Village Goddess.

Buddhism was established by Asoka as the state religion of nearly all India, including the Indo-Gangetic plain; and Jainism spread even further south. Both the Saivite and Vaishnavite creeds owed their victory over Buddhism and Jainism to energetic propaganda, combined with a more effective appeal, both to the popular mind, which naturally preferred anthropomorphic deities surrounded by innumerable myths to the philosophic atheism of the Buddhist creed, and also to the Brahman caste, to whom the privileges of hereditary priesthood were more attractive than Buddhist celibacy and austerity. The propaganda naturally took the form of the greatest possible exaltation of the deities.

The orographical conditions of India, the lack of any natural frontier divisions of the great northern plain, and its preponderance in natural wealth and population over the rest of India, early led to the establishment of great empires, separated from one another in time by periods of warfare and disorder. All thinking men, other than those who lived by war, saw the need for unification in political organisation. This attitude of mind was paralleled by the tendency of religious thinkers to aim at unification of deities. The logical Indian mind carried out this process to its full completion. Not only are all the deities, of whatever origin or sex, only different names and varying conceptions of the one and only God, but all matter and all living creatures are nothing but illusory forms behind which the one and only God is the sole Reality.

Magical ideas have lost very little of their ancient power. The beneficial effect of wearing gold, silver, and precious stones is undoubted; distinguished university graduates have assured me that snake bite is effectually cured by the utterance of *mantrams*. Recently an Ayurvedic physician was brought before the Presidency court for manslaughter, he had dosed a patient with corrosive sublimate and she had died. His defence was that he had "killed the poison with *muppu*." The magistrate had to adjourn the case to hiscover what *muppu* was. He consulted ᴛhe editor of the new Tamil dictionary, who in turn consulted his pundits. They told him that *muppu*=*munru uppu*, three salts, and assured him that if *muppu* was properly prepared, with the right *mantrams* rightly pronounced, and taken undiluted, it would turn to gold the inside of the person who swallowed it, and he would never die; but if mixed with any poison, all the injurious qualities of the poison would be neutralised, and it would become a useful medicine. The unfortunate physician must have made a mistake in the preparation of his *muppu*. Another specially valuable drug is known to Indian medicine. If administered with the right ceremonies and *mantrams* it restores the dead to life. Admittedly this drug is seldom used, and for a good reason. If the slightest mistake is made either in performing the necessary ceremonies, or in repeating the appropriate *mantrams*, the dead man stays dead, and the physician himself dies.

In the year 1920, when the bridge over the River Cooum, in Madras, hard by Government House, was being widened, so general was the belief that a human sacrifice was necessary that a Government servant who was carrying a little boy, his own son, through a street in Georgetown was set upon and murdered by a mob believing that he had kidnapped the boy under Government orders to be the victim.

The broad principles both of contagious and of sympathetic magic could only, as it seems to me, have been deduced by hard thinking. For this reason I regard it as more probable that the theory of magic was worked out originally in Egypt only, and thence spread by slow diffusion all over the world, than that it was the spontaneous production of local thought in many places. But if the hypothesis of diffusion from one centre only be correct, yet if, as appears to be the case, Palæolithic man of the Aurignacian culture in Europe left clear evidence of his belief in magic, the diffusion must have been so early that both Dravidians and Aryans must have possessed it before Vedic times. But as the Vedas attribute special magical powers to the Dravidians, and in particular the power of raising the dead, Indian magic of the present day must be regarded as a Dravidian rather than an Aryan contribution to Indian culture.

CHAPTER V

THE ECONOMIC BASIS OF DRAVIDIAN CULTURE

RICE growing is obviously the economic basis of Dravidian culture. Many sorts of millets are grown in addition to rice, but only as a *pis aller*, and the ploughs and other implements used for cultivating the millets are borrowed from rice cultivation, for which they are much more suitable.

It has been suggested that rice growing was introduced into India by the Dravidians from a supposed place of origin somewhere in Turkestan. This appears improbable, not only because Turkestan is an unlucky choice for the first home of the Dravidians, but also because, if the Dravidians had developed rice cultivation in the district which they inhabited before entering India, they would probably have settled down in that spot, and not have emigrated in a body, leaving no traces behind. It is more reasonable to suppose that the migration took place while they had the mobility characteristic of non-agricultural peoples. Wild rice is indigenous in various parts of India, and is still part of the subsistence of some castes in the south-west, and there is no botanical difficulty in the supposition that the cultivated varieties, proverbially said to be as numerous as the days of the year, have been derived from the Indian wild variety.

It is probable, though not certain, that the cultivation of barley and millet in Egypt antedates the cultivation of rice in India, and therefore it may well be, as is maintained by Perry in " The Children of the Sun," that the idea of cereal cultivation was imported into India from Egypt although the grain cultivated was native. It is equally possible that rice cultivation preceded the establishment of sea communication between the two countries. Again, as suggested above by Fleure, it may have come overland at a very early date from Mesopotamia. So far as I know there is no direct evidence bearing with any certainty upon the question. But it is a striking fact that close resemblances in all sorts of culture elements between India and other countries which derived the "heliolithic" culture, probably from Egypt, are found much less frequently among the Dravidians of South India than among tribes speaking languages of the Munda group, and their neighbours in North-east India who, though they may speak Tibeto-Burman or even Dravidian languages, are of similar culture to the Mundaris, and perhaps of the same race, like the Oraons, Khasis, Angamis, and other sections of Nāgas. Since it is the south of India which came most directly into connection with Egypt this fact appears to me to be an example of the general law expounded by W. H. R. Rivers in "The Contact of Peoples" (Essays and studies presented to William Ridgeway): "The extent of the influence of one people upon another depends on the difference in the level of their cultures." The cause of the relative slightness of the visible signs of heliolithic influence upon Tamils and Malayalis may very probably have been that as they had independently made the all-important advance from being food-gatherers to food-producers, they had relatively little to learn from "The Children of the Sun," and therefore were less disposed to imitate the practices of the foreign teachers in detail. At the present day the great difficulty for India in the adoption of elements of Western civilisation, even where the advantage is manifest, is not in learning new things, but in unlearning old.

Assuming the Dravidians did discover for themselves the art of paddy cultivation, possibly Grant Allen's brilliant suggestion with regard to the origin of cultivation is true in their case, the suggestion, namely, that it began with the placing of seeds, besides the corpse when it was buried, for the use of the dead man, and that this is the explanation of the close connection between primitive agriculture and human sacrifice. But on the whole I am disposed to think that the first agricultural operation applied to paddy cultivation was not sowing but transplantation; young plants of wild paddy being taken by still nomadic groups from one swamp to another when it became advisable to move to new hunting grounds, or gathered from distant and inconvenient spots to be re-planted as near as possible to settlements. The clearing out of weeds to make room for the new plants would naturally follow immediately, and the accidental dropping of rice seeds in places and at times favourable to growth might have been the origin of the art of making seed beds.

We are on surer, and also on more fruitful ground, when we turn from the possible origins of paddy cultivation to its influence on Dravidian, and consequently on Indian culture.

Much of India, including particularly those parts which have had a dominating influence on the evolution of Indian social life, comes under the description of Fleure's "Lands of Increment." In the upper basin of the Ganges, the deltaic areas of the Brahmaputra, Ganges, Mahanadi, Godavari, Kistna, Palar, North and South Pennar and Cauvery, and on the low lands of the Malabar coast, there was, until the excessive growth of population brought the economic Law of Diminishing Returns into operation, a lavish return to a comparatively slight amount of human effort. At the same time the damp heat of the climate makes muscular effort generally disagreeable, but facilitates the continuous thinking and speculation that requires bodily quiescence, and reduces to a minimum the need for food and clothing. Hence there has been, ever since the agricultural stage was reached, a great desire to live without manual labour, combined with exceptional scope for such an existence. We find, for example, that in the district of Trichinopoly and neighbouring districts a Brahman family of moderate size possessed of as little as five acres of paddy land of medium quality can, and ordinarily does, live in idleness on the produce, the land being cultivated by Pallans or Paraiyans ; and, in the specially rich valley of the River Tambraparni, three acres are enough to support a family in idleness.

Moreover, in India Nature is peculiarly terrible as well as exceptionally bounteous. Storms, rain, sunshine, in equal degree, operate with magnificent intensity. The uric acid diseases which cripple and plague, but take an unconscionable time in killing us, are little to be feared, diseases which kill within a few days, or even a few hours, are rife. And there is always the terrible uncertainty of the monsoons, for even in those districts where the rain never fails it may come, as on the Malabar coast, at the wrong time, or, as in Bengal, in such abundance as to produce devastating floods.

These geographical and geographico-economic conditions produce their appropriate social consequences as follows :—

(1) The priestly class, claiming the pos-

session of power to control Nature directly by magical arts or indirectly by propitiation of deities, tends continually to rise to a position of supreme power and influence. Warfare may from time to time, in this area or that, temporarily over-ride this tendency by giving military chieftains predominance, but such effects have been evanescent.

(2) The priestly class uses its power to emancipate itself from manual toil, but to a considerable extent utilises its time and energy for mental activity.

(3) But being exempt from the necessity of manual labour, and having less need than in other countries for the produce, in food and clothing, of manual labour, it tends to expend its mental activity to a very slight degree only on the improvement of agricultural and industrial methods and apparatus, or on the supervision of agricultural and industrial operations, and to a much larger degree on speculation into the nature of man and the universe and the ultimate causes of phenomena. The priestly class therefore tends to be the

intellectual class, and an intellectual class with a specially strong bias towards the building up of elaborate systems on insufficient bases of fact, and a disinclination to test its deductions by practical experience.

(4) The feeling that the intellectual class should do very little or no manual work leads to the feeling that the manual labour class should do little or no thinking.

These effects are intensified by the operation of the principle of hereditary occupations, and by the caste system, which is further examined below.

For the next stage in this survey we must consider separately the matrilinear and patrilinear sections of the Dravidians of South India.

Among the Malayalis of the west coast inheritance of property in the female line and reckoning of kinship through the mother prevail among the most numerous castes, Nayars, Bants, Tiyyas, and others, and to some extent among the Syrian Christians. Among other Dravidians the ordinary Hindu law of succession is followed, and kinship is reckoned through both parents, but more especially through the father, a son taking his father's name to precede his own. But among their marriage customs there are various peculiarities which are regarded as sufficient evidence that all Dravidians were originally matrilinear.

The customs of the Nayars may be taken as typical of matrilinear castes and briefly described. The joint undivided family prevails, called *tarvad*. The *tarvad* holds its property jointly, the family house and lands either held directly under Government (Madras Presidency or Cochin or Travancore State) or on lease under a Nambudiri Brahman landlord. All sons of the *tarvad* inherit from their mothers the right to share during their lives in the annual produce, but transmit no rights of inheritance to their children; the daughters both inherit in the same manner, and transmit the same rights to their children. The eldest woman of the *tarvad* is its titular head; the eldest man usually, with the title of *Karanavan*, is entrusted with the actual management of the property, but sometimes he is displaced by a younger man regarded as more competent.

It is the duty of the Nayar mother to arrange a ceremonial marriage for each daughter before puberty. The ceremony is brief, simple, and inexpensive; the essential part being the tying of the bridal necklace round the neck of the girl. The ceremonial bridegroom may be a complete stranger, a mere passer-by, to whom the mother gives a rupee for obliging. He acquires no marital rights or privileges, goes away immediately, and probably never sees the girl again. Later on the girl manages her own real matrimonial affairs at her own discretion. The matrimonial tie is called *sambandham*, which may be a lifelong monogamous marriage, or a very temporary alliance. The woman may terminate the connection whenever she chooses, but she may only enter into *sambandham* with one man at a time; the man is under no such restrictions. In Malabar the women continue to live in their own *tarvads,* and are visited there by their partners, and the dissolution of *sambandham* takes place either by the woman intimating to her lover that he must cease his visits, or by the man ceasing them of his own accord. The children are, of course, the children of their mother's *tarvad*, and their father has no responsibility towards them. All his responsibilities to the next generation are on behalf of the children of his own *tarvad,* that is his sisters' children, and the children of other women of his *tarvad* who are practically in the relationship of sisters to him.

But if a Nayar goes away from his home and acquires property by his own exertions, he is recognised as having individual ownership of that property, and can bequeath it to whom he likes. The management of the *Karanavans* tends to be slack, and on the average the value of the property of a *tarvad* does not increase from generation to generation; but the numbers to be maintained often do, until the *tarvad* becomes unable to support them all. Many young men therefore are compelled to abandon the easy life, which in a prosperous *tarvad* consists mainly of eating, drinking, sleeping, and courting, by the sheer impossibility for the *tarvad* of supplying food enough to keep all its members alive. Others, without compulsion, are prompted by ambition to go in quest of a career. When such young men have succeeded in establishing themselves in other parts of India they modify the usual form of *sambandham* by taking away their partners from their *tarvads*, to live with them in the homes which they have provided; the right on either side to terminate the *sambandham* remains in theory, but lapses in practice, and the father leaves the property which he has acquired to his own children.

It is evident that the *tarvad*, and its system of inheritance, called *marumakkattayam*, is economically disadvantageous and is doomed to disappear. The relatively high status and measure of independence it allows women weighs heavily on the credit side, but it is possible that this social merit of the institution will not be lost, and that the social and matrimonial institutions of the matrilinear castes of the west coast will become assimilated to those of Burma rather than to those of the rest of India.

The earliest European observers guessed that the *tarvad* was a political institution devised by military chieftains, like the Zamorin of Calicut, in order that there might be a great force of young men available for enlistment untroubled by family ties. On this theory the ceremonial marriage of girls before puberty would be a survival from the time when such marriages were real. But there can be no doubt that the *tarvad*, *marumakkattayam* and *sambandham* are the earlier customs, which have been superseded generally in India by patriarchal customs, but have survived on the west coast as a result of conditions specially favourable to their conservation. We have, then, to enquire what these special conditions are.

Following Hartland, we may take it as proved that kinship was originally reckoned through the mother only. Before the first pioneers of civilisation entered upon the agricultural stage there was little property to inherit; that little property consisting of tools and implements of various kinds. Hence the original custom of inheritance must necessarily have been that the tools or weapons used by men, if not buried with them, were inherited by other men, and those used by women passed to other women. What relationship male heirs commonly bore to the dead man need not concern us here; but obviously whatever tools a woman left would naturally pass to her daughters. When these pioneers of civilisation added cultivation to their activities as a supplement to the chase, fishing, and gathering of wild fruits and roots, the new work was undoubtedly assigned to the women, and therefore the ownership of the agricultural tools, of the growing plants, and, as soon as ownership in land was recognised, the ownership of the little cultivated plots, would naturally be regarded as being vested in the women, and descending by inheritance from mother to daughter. As long as hunting was the mainstay this arrangement would be secure. As soon as the population depended mainly upon agriculture, and the men as well as the women worked in the fields, the social equilibrium became unstable, but might still be maintained for many generations, as it was in Egypt and Mesopotamia, until some sort of shock led the men to question its reasonableness. This might come through war, or conceivably through contact with peoples who passed directly from the hunting to the pastoral stage, and among whom the hereditable property from the beginning was held by the men, or perhaps merely from the pressure of increasing population upon the land, leading to the extension of cultivation into more difficult areas which from the beginning were cleared and cultivated by the men.

If this argument be sound the circumstances specially favouring the survival of inheritance from mother to daughter on the Malabar coast are :—

(1) The fact that the cultivated land lay along a narrow strip of territory between seas and backwaters full of fish on the west, and forests abounding in game on the east.

(2) Until comparatively recent times the sea and the mountains effectively sheltered this favoured strip of land from foreign invasions.

(3) The coco-nut palm, which only needs to be planted, and will bear fruit for a hundred years, without ceasing or failing, and yield ripe nuts for about ten months every year, simplified the problem of winning subsistence from the soil with little exertion.

These conditions, however, would not have sufficed. What has maintained the custom of *marumakkattayam* among the Nayars is the manner in which it is dovetailed into the institutions of the Nambudiri Brahmans.

Among the Dravidians, as among other people, the magical and priestly functions were mainly exercised by men, and the privileges and wealth obtainable by the exercise of those functions mostly monopolised by men. It was therefore inevitable that the Nambudiris, like other Brahmans, should early institute for themselves patrilinear descent and inheritance. On the east coast it would appear that the Brahmans encouraged these institutions among other castes. But the Nambudiris apparently aimed at, and effectively achieved, an arrangement leading to the establishment of great and ever-growing family estates. Among them only the eldest son may marry within the caste. All the other sons enter into *sambandham* relations with Nayar women, and the influence of the Brahman caste is exerted to make the Nayar women regard *sambandham* with a Brahman as more honourable and desirable than with a Nayar. The children of these unions, of course, become members of their mothers' *tarvads.*

The Nambudiri who may marry is allowed several Nambudiri wives, but nevertheless a considerable proportion of Nambudiri women do not marry, and these spinsters are kept in rigorous seclusion, particularly from men of their own caste. It is the Nambudiri tradition to acquire land whenever possible but never to part with it. A Nambudiri estate commonly consists of a home farm, cultivated under the supervision of the family, and of lands leased out for periods of twelve years to leaseholders known as *kanomdars*, who are usually the representatives of Nair *tarvads*. If the lease is terminated at the end of the twelve years the *kanomdar* is entitled to compensation for improvements. The *kanomdar* usually sublets the greater part of his holding to men of inferior castes on annual tenancies. Obviously this extreme form of primogeniture among the Nambudiris would break down under the demands of younger sons if it were not for the license allowed to them by the *marumakkattayam* institutions of the Nayars.

The influence of the survival of matrilinear inheritance on the Malabar coast on South Indian social and political life is perceptible. Nayar and Syrian Christian[1] girls supply a very large proportion of the membership of the two women's colleges in Madras, and carry off even a larger proportion of the honours. They also supply a considerable part of the membership of the Maharaja's College at Trivandrum, and compete on level terms with the men. Under the new constitution for India the question whether women should exercise the franchise having been left to the provincial legislatures to decide, the legislative Council for Madras, after a few hours' debate, resolved on doing so by a three to one majority; the Council of Bombay passed a similar resolution, but only by a small majority after two days' debate; Bengal and the other Councils either rejected resolutions in favour of

[1] Among the Syrian Christians (*i.e.* the Indian Christians of the ancient church established in India before A.D. 200) the *marumakkattayam* system of inheritance is still the rule.

women's suffrage or declined even to debate the question. There are, of course, other factors behind this great difference between the north and south of India in the status of women, the relatively slight influence of Mohammedanism in the south being one; but the greater freedom and higher status of women on the Malabar coast certainly has an important influence on the status of women in South India generally.[1]

In Sir Sankaran Nair the Nayar caste has supplied one of the most forceful personalities to Indian political life; but the career of the late Dr T. M. Nair shows more directly the influence of the caste environment. His greatest service to India was the determined fight he put up against a reactionary majority on the Freer-Smith Factories Committee, 1906 to 1908, with the result that the Factories Act of 1911 was based more on his very able dissenting minute than on the report of the majority,

[1] In Burma, however, it was taken as a matter of course that women should have votes on the same terms as men.

and all his proposals that were rejected in 1911 were accepted in 1922. He also founded and organised the non-Brahman political party, which triumphed after his death in the first election for the Madras Legislative Council, and he prompted the starting of the non-Brahman organ, *Justice*, which has a Nayar editor.

The exceptional bounty of Nature on the Malabar coast makes a very short average day's work sufficient to maintain the population according to the different standards of comfort of the different classes. It also makes possible an extreme degree of social inequality ; and actually, perhaps as many as nine-tenths of the adult population do no productive work at all, and the one-tenth who maintain the whole by their labour get only the barest minimum of subsistence and, by way of thanks, are treated as untouchable. On the whole they are said to be more contented than the labouring class of any other country, because it has not occurred to them that any variation in their condition is possible. But even in their case the democratic idea has begun to work. In places they have recently demanded the right to walk along the public high roads even when other people are also using them, and to make purchases in the bazaars. Yet within living memory they were slaves.

In the Carnatic the dependence of the population is more exclusively upon rice and other cereals, and the necessity for labour greater; and it is, of course, greater still on the tableland of the Deccan.

The manner in which rice growing has determined the evolution of Dravidian culture on the deltaic plains of the Carnatic may be illustrated by noting both the resemblances and contrasts between these rice growers and those of China. In both we note the undivided patriarchal family, though in India it breaks up more readily than in China; in both marriages take place at an early age, and are arranged by the parents, though the age is earlier in India; in both a young wife is the servant of her mother-in-law, but more emphatically so in China; in both land is regarded as primarily the property of the family, individual owners having only a life interest, and no power of bequest, though in India British rule has given the individual power to sell or mortgage; in both the rights of ownership vested in individuals and families are limited by the rights of the State, which have decayed in both, but less in India than in China.

Among the points of contrast we may select first for consideration this one—China is peculiarly the land of filial piety, India is the land of spoiled children. We all know the story of the middle-aged Chinaman who wept when his old mother thrashed him, not because her blows hurt, but because their lightness showed that her arm was getting feeble. Against this place the true story of an old lady of a village in the district of Coimbatore. Being old and feeble, and conscious that her services to her son no longer recompensed him for the expense of maintaining her, she proposed to him that he should free himself of the burden by killing her, and suggested that she might then be of some use if he so disposed of her corpse as to make her death a basis for a charge of murder against some villager who belonged to the opposite faction.[1]

One does not need to land in India to observe the intense Indian fondness for children. It is visible in the eyes of the Lascars watching the children on board ship. The Emperor Akbar is reported to have said that every man ought to have four wives, a Persian to converse with, a Hindu to look after the children, a Mongol to do the work, and a Tartar to be beaten when the others misbehaved. Love of children is one of the commonest motifs of Dravidian poetry. The following example is as nearly literal a translation as possible of a Tamil poem, the order of the original being followed :—

" The touch of little feet that dabble in the mud,
Of little hands still sticky with sweet food,

[1] For a further illustration of village faction-intrigue see the note at the end of this chapter.

Of breasts still wet with dribblings from wee mouths
And lotus-petal-rosy infant lips—
The clambering grip of his own little sons—
Whose body has not thrilled to these delights,
He, we shall say, has not the body of a man.

The tinkling of the anklets' gems and gold
Worn on the feet, fair as the soft spring leaves,
Of toddling children, and the lisping words
From lips red as the scented water lily—
Whose ear has not drunk in the nectar of these sounds.
His ear, we say, is like a wooden doll's."

That Solomon said, in accents mild, "Spare the rod and spoil the child," proves to the Tamilian that his reputation for wisdom was undeserved. The proper way to manage children is to tell them stories, and that is, perhaps, the reason why India is peculiarly the country of popular fiction. I first came across this fact, familiar to every British mother who employs an ayah, when, a day or two after my arrival in Madras, a student of the Presidency College, who was showing me how to distinguish the larvæ of the *anopheles* and other malaria-carrying mosquitos from the more innocent varieties which also breed abundantly in the " silver Cooum " which flows through the middle of the city, rushed away to keep a promise to tell fairy tales to his little niece.

With regard to China, M. Edmond Demolins and others of the continuators of Leplay hold that the Chinese evolved their singularly perfect, but singularly laborious system of cultivation in Kan-Su and the Wei-ho valley, cultivating millet at first and rice as they reached the plains. Success depended on careful irrigation ; a sufficiency of food could only be obtained by making small areas yield to the utmost. So to this day the Chinese peasant families treat each rice plant with individual care ; when the time for transplantation comes each root is handled separately, and dipped into a vessel of liquid manure before it is placed in its proper hole. Wheat is treated similarly. The yield per acre puts Europe to shame, but this result demands the labour of many hands ; little hands will serve, but they must be careful. Hence

Chinese agriculture depends upon the organised and disciplined labour of little children, and children are disciplined accordingly. They must learn from the cradle that zealous effort to carry out perfectly the wishes of their parents is the object of their lives. There is no doubt about these social facts whatever may be the truth of the geographical explanation offered.

No such severe discipline has been imposed on the Indian people by their environment. The cultivation of rice is less careful and elaborate. In some districts it is sown broadcast, and not transplanted. As a rule transplantation is done somewhat carelessly, and it is done by adults, mostly women. Single transplantation has been introduced by the Madras Agricultural Department, and is slowly spreading, but the landholders who adopt it get it done by hired women coolies. In poor families naturally children early learn to help their parents, but the helping largely takes the form of scampering about on wastes and common pastures, keeping an eye on goats or cows, and having a good time. Dogs, by the way, also are little disciplined, and apart from certain breeds of hunting dogs, South Indian dogs seem to be kept by their owners merely to bark.

The economic basis both of Indian and of Chinese culture then is rice cultivation; but while the psychological basis of Chinese society is filial obedience, acquired by the training of peasant families in steady and meticulous industry, that of Indian society is the humble and conscientious obedience paid by the castes of manual workers to their superiors, and the reverence paid by all other castes to the priestly intermediaries between humanity and the gods.

NOTE

VILLAGE FACTION

"I ONCE, and only once," said an Indian Civil servant, now retired, "came across an instance of an Indian vakil throwing up a case rather than accept a fee for defeating justice.

"I was then a Deputy Collector in Tinnevelly. In a certain village in that district, divided as is common in Tinnevelly into two factions, feeling was running high. Faction A held an excited meeting by night. It was unanimously agreed that faction B was getting unbearable, and that something must be done about it. Various schemes having been discussed, it was further agreed that a false accusation of murder should be brought against two leading members of faction B. A young man called Guruswami was present, and it was pointed out to him that he had an old father who was of little use, and who might well be sacrificed to the common cause and provide the necessary victim. Guruswami promised to kill his father, and hand over the corpse to be used according to the plan agreed upon. But after he got home he changed his mind. A second even more excited meeting was held, and great pressure was put upon Guruswami to make him keep the contract, but he refused obstinately. However, a more complaisant young man was found who also had an aged father, and that same night the substitute for Guruswami's father was killed and placed in the village street in front of a house belonging to one of the members of this same faction A, and there at dawn other members duly discovered it and informed the police. A Eurasian policeman was sent to investigate. Two members of the faction A deposed that being in the house above mentioned late at night, at work on accounts by lamplight, they had looked out and seen the murder committed by two named members of faction B. The policeman, being for a policeman a man of unusual penetration, examined the room in which the witnesses alleged that they were sitting, and observed that the lamp said to have been used gave a very feeble light, that the night had been very dark, and that from the window, even by daylight, only the feet of a man standing on the spot where the murder was alleged to have taken place would have been visible.

"Then faction A perceived that the matter was not going to proceed quite as smoothly and easily as they had anticipated. They felt they must have skilled assistance to see the case through. They went to my friend ——, who already, though young, had a rising reputation. They explained the whole situation to him, promised him a handsome fee, and were both astonished and disgusted when he refused to take up the case. They took it to an older and more experienced vakil, a member of the Madras

Legislative Council, whose ideas on professional ethics were less eccentric. He came down and held a consultation with the faction leaders. What passed can only be guessed. But after the consultation one member of faction A went to Madras and bought a new lamp of high power, and two others, being masons, so altered the window that the whole scene of the murder could easily have been seen from it if it had occurred as alleged.

"The trial of the two accused men then took place, and the accusers triumphantly produced the lamp and exhibited the window. But the Eurasian policeman, unfortunately, was a man of unusual discretion as well as unusual penetration. When originally called in, he had made exact records of the description of the lamp and of the height and size of the window, and had put these on record in the police station. So the case broke down, the two accused men were acquitted, and the police prosecuted the accusers for the fabrication of a false charge. When matters reached this point I was transferred to another district, so that I missed the conclusion. But that is the only instance I know of a vakil refusing a case out of love of justice."

CHAPTER VI

SOME FEATURES OF DRAVIDIAN CULTURE

THAT caste is a Dravidian institution has been pointed out above, and though it pervades all India it is best studied in the south. The material has been admirably put together in Thurston's great work, "Castes and Tribes of Southern India." A perusal, or even a partial perusal of that book will, I anticipate, convince any enquirer that neither of the well-known theories of the origin of caste is sufficient, but that they must be combined. In other words, the origin lies partly in occupational, partly in racial differences.

In all early civilisations, and even to a large extent at the present day, there is a decided tendency for occupations to become hereditary; the son of a Durham coal-miner, for example, probably becomes a coal-miner; the son of a Norfolk agricultural labourer an agricultural labourer, and the former probably marries the daughter of another Durham coal-miner, and the latter the daughter of a Norfolk agricultural labourer. If this tendency were to become absolutely dominant, so that the Durham boy could only become a coal-miner, and was permitted to marry no one but a coal-miner's daughter, coal-mining would become a caste like the caste of goldsmiths, or masons, of South India.

We are naturally led, then, to regard such occupational castes as originating from the tendency of a son to follow his father's calling; but we have to ask how it is that in India alone the full development should have taken place. The explanation may be as follows.

There is first the antiquity and long, slow development of Dravidian civilisation. One art after another became developed into the exclusive occupation of certain artisans, who jealously kept their methods as exclusive possessions as possible in their own families. The tropical climate imposes inertia, and hinders that more energetic frame of mind which seeks for more than one occupation, so that in India the artisan tends to be more specialised than in temperate regions, a fact which is very apparent in domestic service. The tropical climate also leads to early sexual maturity, and that again to marriages of boys and girls who are still immature in every other respect. The Indian lad, in consequence, normally becomes a husband and a father when still only a half-trained apprentice to his father. Naturally in these circumstances it is his father who selects his bride for him, and naturally he selects the bride from the families of men who follow the same craft. The association of magical practices and religious ceremonies with the work of the craft helps in the building up of caste solidarity. Marriage outside the caste becomes one of the things which are not done, and therefore reprehensible.

The facts (1) that Indians generally regard the caste system as essentially an early device to secure a certain degree of division of labour, technical training, and development of aptitude for particular crafts; (2) that new castes tend to arise in consequence of changes in methods of industry; and (3) that the caste system is most highly developed in those parts of India in which the ancient Dravidian culture has been least affected by foreign invasion, all point to the conclusion that the system had its original root in the causes stated above. Nevertheless, it is very plain that other forces have operated to produce the caste arrangements now existing, and that these come largely from racial differences. It would appear that the idea and principle of caste having been established at a very early date in the social organisation of the Dravidian people, it so modified the consequences of historic events of very varied character as to make them harmonise with it. Thus, for example, in the process of the wars by which the Andhra or Telugu empire of Vijayanagar was extended southwards, numerous families of the Telugu caste of Reddis were settled in Tamil villages. Had the caste system not existed previously their descendants would in course of time have been merged in the native population. Actually they still remain a distinct caste, retaining the Telugu language and the somewhat fairer complexions and bigger frames which they brought from their original more northern home, by dint of marrying only within the caste. The whole idea of caste is abhorrent to Mohammedanism, which preaches, more effectively than Christianity, the equal brotherhood of all believers. But the South India Mohammedans are just another caste; and so are Europeans and Indian Christians.

The very title of Thurston's book, "Castes *and* Tribes," is suggestive. For among these separate communities there are, on one hand, some like the Kollans (blacksmiths) and Idayans (shepherds), which are occupational castes pure and simple; on the other hand, some, like the Todas, racially distinct from their neighbours, or the Badagas, who have so long been isolated from the rest of their Canarese kinsfolk as to become in effect distinct; and others again with regard to which it is difficult to say whether they are regarded as being properly separate castes or separate tribes; and yet again some who are marked out equally by occupational and racial distinctions, like the "Sourashtra Brahmans," a caste of silk weavers, who came originally from Gujerat, and fleeing from Mohammedan conquest settled in one part of India after another, finally migrating to the extreme south.

The Aryan invasion, though not, as some have supposed, the cause of the caste system, may well have modified it by strengthening two tendencies which were, however, inherent in it: (1) the tendency to associate caste differences with difference of shade of colour; and (2) the tendency for castes to be graded in a fairly definite scale of social precedence. The grading is not quite defined, for numerous cases might be cited of two castes, each of which regards itself as socially superior to the other, but these exceptions are less numerous than might be expected. Thus, for example, the Director of Industries of the state of Travancore recently found that the sawyers earned more money than the carpenters, and the carpenters more than the cabinet-makers, and yet the sawyers were petitioning for technical education in order that they might become carpenters, and the carpenters in order to become cabinet-makers, the change of occupation in each case, while leading to greater poverty, also bringing higher social status.

The prohibition of interdining between different castes appears to follow naturally from the prohibition of intermarriage, meals ordinarily being more private among Indians than with us, and ceremonial feasts being largely associated with births, deaths and marriages. Untouchability in some cases is a natural result of occupation; thus the sanctity of the cow causes the flaying of cattle, and even working up of leather, to be regarded as occupations of a somewhat sinful character, hence the

Chandalas and Chakkiliyans, leather working castes, are untouchable. It is not so easy to see why the great rice-cultivating castes of Paraiyans, Pallans and Cherumas are also untouchable ; but it may be noted that it is only where the geographical conditions make it possible to impose all or nearly all strenuous outdoor labour on a depressed caste, and at the same time intensify the desire to escape such labour, that agricultural labourers are untouchable. Untouchability, once established, tends to justify itself ; the Paraiyan, being untouchable, does not scruple to eat mutton and drink toddy, and neglects various niceties of behaviour regarded as essential in higher castes.

The origin of the Brahman caste must necessarily remain a matter for speculation. But there are indications pointing to a probable hypothesis. Let us modify Elliot Smith's suggestion quoted in Chapter I., "The bringers of the new" (heliolithic) "culture mingled their blood with the aboriginal pre-Dravidian population, and the result was the Dravidians," so as to read, "The bringers of the heliolithic culture from Egypt mingled their blood with the Dravidians, and the result was the Brahman caste." That hypothesis[1] harmonises well with the facts that—

(1) The Brahmans have a tradition of descent from an ancestry different from that of the commonalty. In the south of India they interpret this tradition as indicating that they are of Aryan descent, and other castes of Dravidian descent. This theory has been carelessly accepted by most European writers, but it obviously does not stand examination. It has been accepted because the Brahmans are sufficiently different in facial appearance, complexion, and intellectual habit from the other castes to make the tradition of a racial difference appear probable, and before the publication of the works of Elliot Smith and others along similar lines, it was naturally assumed that any non-Dravidian

[1] Prof. Elliot Smith writes: "I fully agree with the modified form you suggest."

element in Brahman ancestry must have been Aryan.

(2) The carriers of the heliolithic culture, as Perry has shown in "The Children of the Sun," claimed divinity, and established in various places in Indonesia and elsewhere ruling classes claiming divinity or divine descent. It is also the traditional Brahman theory that every Brahman is a god.

(3) The carriers of the heliolithic culture combined the worship of the sun and serpent. The most venerated and most conservative of all Brahman castes, the Nambudiris, have, as mentioned above, as one of their chief functions the worship of cobras in the shrines of Nayar households. If, as suggested above, Brahma is a solar deity, the whole Brahman caste is even more closely associated with sun worship.

(4) The carriers of the heliolithic culture brought from Egypt a knowledge of the arts of spinning and weaving, as well as of agriculture. In other countries to which they brought the first knowledge of these arts, the divine race of Children of the

Sun and the traditional culture heroes are specially associated with agriculture and irrigation. We can trace no such association in India between agriculture and mythical culture heroes; and this confirms the conclusion reached above on other grounds that the Dravidians had begun the cultivation of rice before sea contact with Egypt was established. In these circumstances it would be the arts of spinning and weaving (if not also learnt independently) that would become the most important gifts of the newcomers, and which would be specially associated with the superhuman race originating from unions between the divine strangers and native women. The distinguishing mark of the Brahman is the sacred cotton cord worn by him inside all other clothing. This appears to be a very clear indication that Brahman ascendancy has one of its roots in the descent of Brahmans from foreigners who earned the gratitude and homage of the population of India by teaching them to spin and weave.

It was, of course, the general idea of spinning and weaving that came to India across the sea from Egypt, not the specific art of spinning and weaving cotton. Of that art India was no doubt the first home. In the Telugu country (and perhaps elsewhere) it is a tradition that the sacred thread of the Brahmans must be made of tree cotton. This indicates that tree cotton was used before the lint of the cotton plant, which has now superseded it for practically all purposes except that of stuffing life-saving waistcoats. This inference is supported by the fact that all the most ancient accounts, from Herodotus onwards, of Indian cotton say that it grew on trees, with the result that to this day the German name for cotton is *Baumwolle*, tree-wool.

How ancient the manufacture of silk in India is, whether the art is indigenous, or whether it was introduced from China or from some other foreign country, are questions on which I can offer no opinion. Jute manufacture is doubtless indigenous, the plant itself being scarcely found, even to-day, outside India, but it is impossible to guess when first the people of Bengal began to use it. The same may be said with regard to the use of coir in Malabar, though that is, no doubt, of extreme antiquity.

The very early development of textile industries in India, and the elaboration of the cotton industry in particular by its association with the art of dyeing, necessarily tended to favour specialisation of workers in specific crafts and therefore to strengthen the occupational basis of the caste system. It also, by multiplying desirable commodities, increased wants, and desire for wealth and authority, and so tended to help in the creation of wealthy and privileged classes, government, and the building of capital cities, which, once started, grew by their own centripetal attraction. These results again react on industries, by creating a demand for finer, more elaborate and costly, and more artistic products. The final fruit was the wonderful Dacca muslin, the fame of which entered even into western European fairy tales.

Metal and stone-working industries apparently had an evolution similar to that of textile industries. Assuming the truth of the theory that the motive that sent out the early Egyptian navigators, and their Minoan and Phœnician coadjutors, was the quest for life-giving substances, their most valued finds in India would be the pearls and sacred chank shells of the Gulf of Manaar, and the gold washed down by the streams from the Western Ghats. I cannot, by the way, accept Elliot Smith's suggestion, endorsed by Perry, that gold owed its prestige originally to its being used to make imitation shells. It seems to me that as soon as the idea of contagious magic was established in men's minds the chemical inertness of gold must necessarily have caused men to believe that the wearing of gold would be a preventive of disease. This theory is still practically universal in India.

Perhaps the foreign metal workers were

ignorant of iron, though familiar with copper and bronze; even so they might have been the first to utilise the Indian ore, since, in many parts of India, surface iron ore of very high metal content abounds. Iron implements have been found in the Hyderabad cairns. Both the use of iron and the art of building in stone appear to have been known to the Dravidians in pre-Vedic times. Just as the use of the copper chisel, as Elliot Smith has shown, started the megalithic work of Egypt, so the use of iron probably fostered stone-working in India. The use of iron again tends to foster the manufacture of weapons, the evolution of a military caste, and stronger and more rapacious Governments.

The use of gold and silver, of pearls, diamonds, and other precious stones reacts upon social organisation in a manner similar to the development of textile art, but perhaps even more powerfully. The laws of Manu declare that it is one of the duties of a king to wear precious stones. By the principle of contagious magic the virtue of the stones passes into the monarch, and by the principle of sympathetic magic, since he is the magical symbol of the life of the state, the whole community gains the same benefit. The duty of a king to add to the royal treasures of gems, never parting with them except in dire necessity, rests upon the same basis. And for the ordinary man, the purchase of ornaments of precious metal and precious stones is regarded as the most rational and remunerative form of investment. They yield one income in magical virtue, and another in social prestige, as long as they are worn, and the capital value can always be realised if necessary.

The Indian demand for commodities still runs very much to the two extremes, a demand for the most meagre supply of the most indispensable necessaries for the masses, and a demand for costly luxuries for the very few. What middle-class demand there is, is comparatively recent, but it is growing fast.

CHAPTER VII

THE DRAVIDIAN PROBLEM TO-DAY

In previous chapters we have been concerned with historical problems, who the Dravidians are, to what extent the Indian population is Dravidian by race, and to what extent Indian culture is Dravidian rather than Aryan. The question now to be considered relates to the future. It is, "What special part has that corner of India in which Dravidian speech persists to play in the future history of India and of the world ?"

In viewing the facts of to-day for the purpose of finding an answer to this question, we are struck by a curious contradiction. "Dravida" is at once the part of India where the most ancient culture still survives, and the part which is closest in touch with the twentieth century. In other parts of India one feels oneself sometimes carried back into the Middle Ages, or even into Palestine in the time of the Crusades; in such a temple as that of Menakshi and Siva in Madura one can only dream of having revisited some great shrine of Isis and Osiris in Egypt, or of Marduk in Babylon. But when the officer of the Madras Agricultural Department specially concerned with cattle visited that temple, he found that the sacred Bull, the Indian analogue of the god Apis, was a Jersey.

The social institutions of the Nayars are of the type that the very earliest extant Egyptian literature depicts as there and then disappearing; and a young Nayar the other day was reading a paper to the Royal Asiatic Society on the Indian Labour Problem. Though commercially Madras is in a backwater, as an intellectual port of entry and departure between India and the western world it functions no less actively than Calcutta or Bombay. The refashioning of Indian philosophy to suit the West was carried out on the banks of the Adyar, an ex-schoolmaster of Madras is the brilliantly eloquent representative of India in London and Geneva. In politics, the more picturesque and forceful personalities, Tilak, Gandhi, C. R. Das, belong to other parts of India, but in capacity for working the machinery of representative government the Tamil Brahman is supreme, and to Tamil Brahmans leadership in the Legislative Assembly falls naturally. It is to a Nayar to whom, of all Indians, credit is chiefly due for what has been accomplished in factory legislation. Modern trade-unionism took its rise neither in Bombay nor Calcutta, but in Madras; and the Aluminium Workers' Union in Madras is probably the model trade union of all India. The Co-operative movement also began in Madras, and the Triplicane Urban Co-operative Society and the Mylapore Permanent Fund are conspicuous as perhaps the only two important efforts of Indians to apply Western co-operative methods in trading and banking which were started before Indian Governments took steps to foster Co-operation, and which owe practically nothing to official guidance or help. I may be mistaken, but I feel pretty sure that there are, in proportion to population, more Indians in Madras who play cricket, hockey, tennis, and football than in either Calcutta or Bombay. The Tamil attitude towards British sports is accurately represented by an item in the account given by an old student of Kumbakonam College of a distinguished ex-principal, " He taught us to play football, and we said, 'Are we donkeys that he should want to teach us to kick ?' but now we are very grateful to him." And, as indicated above, in everything that relates to the status, education and activities of women, Dravida is far in advance of the rest of India proper, though not on a level with Burma.

One obvious reason for this curious relative modernity is that British influence has been operating in the Carnatic longer than elsewhere. Something, perhaps, may be allowed for the fact that the establishment of British rule was of very obvious benefit to the inhabitants of the plains as the only effective defence against the Mahrattas and the armies of Mysore under Hyder Ali and Tippu Sahib. Christianity is a much larger factor in the south than the north. By tradition the Indian Church was founded by St Thomas the Apostle, and if the tradition is inaccurate, it is not misleading with respect to the probable date of the first teaching of Christianity in India. The so-called "Syrian Christians" have their stronghold in the States of Travancore and Cochin and neighbouring parts of Madras Presidency. But the greatest importance must be attributed to the wide spread of the English language among all the people of Dravidian vernaculars.

The extent to which English has already become the language of South India is amazing. One of my earliest experiences in the city of Madras was to drift into an open-air meeting addressed by Indian speakers from the north on behalf of the new Hindu University of Benares. The speeches were in English, and a large crowd was listening. One of my last experiences in the same city was to attend a half-yearly meeting of the Triplicane Co-operative Society. I was late and was the only European present, but from the beginning all the proceedings had been in English. Madras, a city with but a few more than half a million inhabitants, maintains no less than six daily newspapers, the *Mail*, *Express*, *Hindu*, *New India*, *Justice*, and *Swarajya*, published in the English language, against one in Tamil and one in Telugu. Is there any other city in the world, let alone another city of only about half a million inhabitants, which can maintain six daily newspapers printed in one and the same foreign language? Or to put the question more accurately, can that language be regarded as foreign which the people chiefly use and use by preference in seeking information on the subjects that interest them? At the height of the Home

Rule agitation it was recorded in *New India* as an item of special interest that a public meeting had been held in Kumbakonam, a city in which there were only four European residents, in which the proceedings were in Tamil and not in English. It was an exceptional patriotic effort, as undoubtedly the speakers, and most of the audience, would have been more at their ease with English. The extension of the teaching of English in schools has not been pushed by Government, which never has as much money as it wants for education, but is the result of a general popular demand. Travancore and Mysore are but little behind the Madras Presidency and Cochin is actually in advance.

All India labours under a very serious disadvantage because the language which is the medium of all higher instruction is different from the language of the home. For the present Dravida suffers least. On the average a student of Madras University saves about a year, as compared with students of other Indian universities, in the time necessarily spent in the preliminary study of English before beginning his chosen course of study. But, on the other hand, the development of Bengali, Hindi, or Urdu into an efficient medium for scientific and general education is a much more hopeful proposition than the modernising of any Dravidian language to attain the same result. Northern India can reasonably hope to make one of its vernaculars the literary and scientific organ of between two and three hundred million people; unification of the language of the masses with the language of the learned in South India is most likely to be reached by the disappearance of the Dravidian vernaculars.

My own feeling on this matter has been that the question whether this disappearance was either desirable or inevitable was one which the Madras Presidency ought to face, and that if after due consideration public opinion resolved that it was neither desirable nor inevitable the necessary steps should be taken to find another solution of the language difficulty. Accordingly, during my short period of service on the Madras Legislative Council, I moved a recommendation for the appointment of a committee to enquire into the possibility and advisability of the adoption of a common script for the vernaculars of the Presidency. I argued that if the Dravidian vernaculars were to survive they must combine their strength. The four principal ones, Tamil, Telugu, Canarese and Malayalim, taken together, are spoken by over sixty million people, a population large enough to support a vigorous literature. Each has a different script, so that at present a book printed in any Dravidian language can appeal only, as a maximum, to the educated section of the eighteen odd millions of Tamilians, or to the somewhat smaller educated section of the twenty-four millions of Telugus. But the four languages are so closely related that if there were only a common script, a book printed in Tamil would be understood without much difficulty by Telugus, Canarese and Malayalis. Further, the adoption of a common script and the publication of books in the common script would tend towards an approximation of the literary forms of the four languages to one another. In addition there would be the advantage that the common script, if a new one, could be made much easier to read and write, and much better adapted to the printing press, type-setting machine and typewriter, than any of the existing ones. My motion was lost by a large majority.

In the main the vote of the majority was probably determined by a sort of sentimental conservatism, the feeling that the existing script of each language was an integral part of the language and that a sort of sanctity was attached to it. In some small degree it might have been due to a feeling that it was desirable that the existing drift towards the supersession of the vernaculars by English should continue. My own experience in this matter was only a feeble echo of that of certain reformers who made strenuous efforts to bring literary Telugu into closer touch with modern spoken Telugu, but who were very bitterly opposed by the majority of Telugu pandits. Such Pyrrhic victories for the linguistic Conservatives tend to consign the languages so defended to the museum.

There are some theorists who hold that there is a sort of natural sympathy between the native genius of any particular community and its traditional speech, so that the development of the power of thought in the young is in some degree crippled when what was originally a foreign language is used as the medium for expression. On general grounds this theory seems to me to exaggerate absurdly the innate and inherited differences of mental constitution between one nation or community and another. On the ground of historical evidence it appears to me to be contradicted by experience. I do not think that the Florentines of the age of Dante would have thought more effectively if the Etruscan language of their ancestors had persisted in Tuscany, nor that the repute of French culture would be higher to-day if the vernaculars of the Belgæ, Galli and Aquitani had never given way to that of Cæsar's legionaries. Of all the Dravidian languages Tamil is the one best fitted to be the instrument of exact thought, but it would, I believe, be the general belief of Tamil graduates that English serves them equally well. And if this be so, the advantage of access to all the thought and literature of the world, to the extent to which it was either originally expressed in English or has been translated, is obviously a decisive consideration. On the whole, therefore, I think that the people of South India are wise in their generation in desiring that their children shall learn English early and master it thoroughly.

Whether the use of this or that language best conduces to effective thinking is an arguable question. Whether Parliamentary institutions are better or worse than a bureaucratic government with foreigners holding the most important posts is another arguable question. But whether anæmia conduces either to sound thinking or to effective action, and whether debilitating diseases are beneficial to any country whatsoever, are not arguable questions. For this reason I myself consider that all the recent events in India which have been trumpeted through the world, the Prince of Wales's visit, the Reform of the Constitution, the Malabar Rebellion, the Khilafat and Non-Co-operation movements, are of less importance than the arrival in Madras of the representatives of the Rockefeller Foundation, and the initiation of the crusade against hookworm. Estimates of the proportion of the population of the Madras Presidency suffering from hookworm vary from 65 to 98 per cent.; and it is only one of a group of diseases, of which malaria is the most important, that do not ordinarily kill the patient quickly, but which cause anæmia, general debility and listlessness, and reduce the whole of the activities of life to a lower level. How is it that while the hope that religion holds out in the West is Eternal Life, in India it is Nirvana? Is not the pessimism bred by debilitating diseases, which are not sufficiently pronounced to be regarded by the inexpert as diseases, at least in part the explanation? Hookworm is singled out by the Rockefeller Foundation as the special object of attack, not because it is the most serious of these diseases, but because of the educational value of the effort to combat it, those habits of sanitary cleanliness which must be learnt in order to prevent reinfection after the cure (which is easy) being of universal value.

He who tries to form an estimate of the quality of manhood of the Dravidian from personal observation should allow for the fact that the great majority of those with whom he comes in contact are sick men, suffering from diseases till recently very little understood, but, when understood, preventable. Nor are indications lacking that Dravidian patriotism will respond to the challenge of this new knowledge, and in no narrow nationalistic spirit, but welcoming help from whatever quarter it comes, as, for example, in the person of Miss Ida Scudder from America and Miss Veerasinghe from Ceylon.

From such a campaign against debilitating diseases India may hope for the multiplication of the average of energy of intellect and will by no inconsiderable factor. That means instead of having a very small surplus of energy over and above what is needed to drag on life from day to day, the total surplus energy of the three hundred millions of Indians could become a mighty force—one of the world's greatest assets, newly realised. That India has much need of the West is evident enough. Its fundamental need is nothing less than a change in habit and method of thinking. India needs to learn to mistrust the method of unaided continuous meditation, and to acquire the habit of testing theory, not merely by preconceived theory, but by actual observation and experiment. Sir J. C. Bose is the great Indian pioneer along this path, and others will follow.

When India has thrown off the physical handicap of anæmia, and the mental handicap of a too one-sided method of thinking, those factors which made India a land of high civilisation while Europe was in the stage of barbarism will no doubt again produce their appropriate effects. The land where a student needs little food, only a shred of clothing, and no artificially warmed rooms, the land peculiarly of subtle philosophy, seems a suitable home for a peculiarly democratic culture marked by cheap and simple living and high thinking. Just in proportion as India gains in self-knowledge and self-assurance we see growing and strengthening an Indian scorn of the too materialistic achievements of Europe and America, of the worship of wealth and of force, and of our failure to attain to peace and harmony either between nations, or between individuals and sections of one and the same nation, or even in our own souls. Ultimately it may be found that the West has as much to learn from India as to teach. But in whichever way the flow of intellectual commerce is moving, the English-speaking Dravidians will supply many of the most active intermediaries.

NOTE

THE WORD "ARYAN" AND THE INDO-GERMANIC LANGUAGES

THE word " Aryan " is frequently used to denominate not merely the invaders of India who introduced the Sanscrit language, but also the ancient tribes which originally spoke the various languages of the Indo-Germanic family, or some even earlier tribe, or group of tribes that spoke the proto-Indo-Germanic whence all the languages of the family are derived. This use of the word appears to me objectionable, as it suggests the idea of a definite Aryan race diffusing Indo-Germanic languages partly by force of multiplying in numbers and spreading into different regions, and partly by conquering other races. But when this idea is hypothetically accepted, and we ask, " Were the Aryans of Mediterranean race? Nordic? Alpine—Armenoid? " and so on, the racial identification in each case becomes impossible.

I do not know whether the suggestion has ever been made, but it appears to me to be possible that proto-Indo-Germanic was essentially the language of the trade route between Mesopotamia and the Baltic coast *via* the Black Sea, the language of the ancient traders in amber, who, no doubt, also taught northern Europe many arts, including the smelting and working of iron. The fact that Lithuanian and Sanscrit are the two languages nearest to the original would thus be accounted for; the contradictions between the evidence for this or that spot as the "Aryan Home" would no longer be a difficulty. Further, the indications point to the conclusion that the agglutinative original speech which we can see as a necessary prelude to the highly inflected ancient Indo-Germanic language was itself the produce of cultured minds, and not the barbarous jargon of nomadic pastoralists. . If this hypothesis be correct, the spread of English into many lands from the ports frequented by British ships would be a modern parallel.

On this Prof. Fleure writes: "I have long wondered whether Semitic was a language hammered out along the trade and nomad route around the 'Fertile Crescent' on the north side of the Arabian desert; if so it has had gifts from all sorts of dialects of that desert, and the regions round, while it has also influenced the language of the regions round. So I would welcome the idea that early Indo-Germanic belonged to the trade and nomad groups between the Dnieper and the Hindu Kush, and that much intercourse rubbed down its difficulties and so made it a language to be learnt far and wide. English, thanks to world trade, is a language which takes up foreign words, and so insinuates itself everywhere far more easily than German, which has tended to be given up by commercial emigrants from

Germany. French persists outside the French Empire only among agriculturists, I fancy. I often think, with Peake, that the Alpine peoples of the Carpato-Russian region have learned Indo-Germanic speech, and have adapted the *q* or *chw* or *k* sound characteristic of the short-lipped, long-headed horseman of the plain into the *p* which the Slavonic languages have developed so much, and which is appropriate to the long-lipped broad-headed people. I believe Dr Sampson has somewhat similar views about dialectal divisions among the Gipsies. Throughout this letter I am merely making suggestions, prompted by racial research it is true, but intruding into a field of which I know little."

BIBLIOGRAPHY

Archæological Survey of India.

Asiatic Society of Bengal (Calcutta), Journal, Memoirs and Proceedings.

Baluchistan District Gazetteers.

British Association, Proceedings. Liverpool, 1923.

Bulletin of the Madras Government Museum.

Caldwell, R. Comparative Grammar of the Dravidian Languages. London, 1875.

Cambridge Ancient History. Cambridge, 1923.

Hartland, E. S. Primitive Paternity. London, 1909.

Jastrow, M. (jun.) The Book of Job. Philadelphia, 1920.

Journal of the Royal Anthropological Institute, 1916 and following years.

Journal of the Royal Asiatic Society.

L'Anthropologie. Paris.

Logan, W. Malabar, Madras, 1887.

Man, Royal Anthropological Institute.

Mukerjee, R. Foundations of Indian Economics. London, 1916.

Oldham, C. F. The Sun and the Serpent. London, 1905.

Perry, W. J. The Children of the Sun. London, 1923.

The Relationship between the Geographical Distribution of Megalithic Monuments and Ancient Mines.

Rivers, W. H. R. The Contact of Peoples (Essays and Studies presented to William Ridgeway). Cambridge, 1913.

Ruggeri, G. Outlines of a Systematic Anthropology of Asia. Calcutta, 1921.

Schoff, W. The Periplus of the Erythræan Sea, 1912.

Sewell, R. A Forgotten Empire (Vijayanagar). London, 1900.

Slater, G. Some South Indian Villages. Oxford, 1918.

Smith, G. Elliot. The Ancient Egyptians and the Origin of Civilisation. London, 1923.

The Migrations of Early Culture. Manchester, 1915.

Ancient Mariners, Journal of the Manchester Geographical Society, 1917.

Spencer, B. and Gillen, F. J. The Northern Tribes of Central Australia. London, 1924.

Thurston, E. Castes and Tribes of Southern India. Madras, 1909.

Whitehead, H. (Bishop of Madras). The Village Deities of South India. Madras, 1907.

INDEX